Praise for Jen Singer and **MommaSaid.net**

"I laughed so hard I almost woke up my boys - God forbid."
~ Lisa Merritt, Hammond, Indiana

"I found you because a local gal won your 'Housewife' Award. I stayed because you have a nice site. Thank you for your effort to make our lives as moms a little easier and a little happier."
~ Dawn-Marie Cornett, Ithaca, New York

"Last night after finally getting my two-year-old and four-month-old to bed, I sat down to read an issue of *American Baby* magazine. I have to tell you that your article, 'And What Do You Do?' made me laugh out loud. How many times have I had these same thoughts? Thanks for the laugh!"
~ Anna Stanley, Knoxville, Tennessee

"I am soon to be a stay at home mom ... I am finally quitting my part-time job to be a full time mommy. I saw your site mentioned in *The New York Times*, and have sincerely enjoyed reading it this week, as I brace myself for the change. Thanks for the laughs.
~ Kim O'Connor, New York City

"I just wanted to let you know that your site is hysterically funny some of the best stuff I have read in ages. Thanks for the smile, the snicker, the snort and the guffaw! I will be visiting often!"
~ Chris Sofge, Harrogate, England

"Thank you so much for making a web page that caters to us wonderful people who have given up our pre-existing lives to raise the future of our world. I guess it never dawned on me that I wasn't alone ... until I heard about your web page (thanks *Parenting* magazine)! What a relief to hear funny anecdotes and stories of other moms' misfortunes and blunders and know that somewhere out there is another soul who doesn't always know exactly what they are doing ... It all feels a little (lot) overwhelming at times and I felt the need to thank you."
~ Stacy Theberge, Methuen, Massachusetts

"I am a soon-to-be stay-at-home mommy, and since I live far from family and friends, a good smile will definitely make my day as I enjoy my husband and my first child. This is such an adorable website that will make even the grumpiest of moms crack a smile."
~ Tiffany Ansari, Fords, New Jersey

"I really love this website. Thanks for being so creative. It is so wonderful to take a moment out of my busy days and log onto your website. It is refreshing and delightful."
~ Julie McDaniel, Tallahassee, Florida

"I was a stay-at-home mom many years ago when it was actually accepted. I think your website is great. I could have used it 20 years ago, but I can still relate to some of the funny stories you tell."
~ Linda Arentowicz, Long Valley, New Jersey

"My mom sent an article about the website that had run in the *Huntsville Times* (Alabama). It arrived on a day that I REALLY needed a laugh. Thanks for being a voice for all of us."
~ Dawn Bragg, Germantown, Tennessee

"This is really nice! It's so fun to read stay-at-home mom stories. I feel so isolated most days, a laugh here and there will really pick me up."
~ Summer Christian, Eliot, Maine.

"Just thought I'd let you know that I had a few minutes to check out your website. What started as a 'few minutes' turned into an hour and a half! I started reading and COULD NOT STOP!"
~ Caty Schrope, Kinnelon, New Jersey

14 Hours 'Til Bedtime
A Stay-at-Home Mom's Life in 27 Funny Little Stories

14 HOURS 'TIL BEDTIME:
A Stay-at-Home Mom's Life in 27 Funny Little Stories

by Jen Singer
© 2004, Jennifer Singer

Some of the content previously appeared in *American Baby, Family Circle, The New York Times, Nick Jr., Parenting* and *Woman's Day.*

Author, Jen Singer
www.mommasaid.net

Editor, Terry Doherty
www.thereadingtub.com

Illustrations, Michael Moran
www.mikemoranonline.com

Cover Layout, Wendy Perry
www.littlefingerslittletoes.net

Interior Layout, Nancy Cleary
www.wymacpublishing.com

Published by Wyatt-MacKenzie Publishing, Inc.
15115 Highway 36, Deadwood, Oregon 97430

Printed in the United States of America

14 Hours 'Til Bedtime
A Stay-at-Home Mom's Life in 27 Funny Little Stories

by Jen Singer

Wyatt-MacKenzie Publishing, Inc.
DEADWOOD, OREGON

For my mom, who was class mother for eleven years.

ACKNOWLEDGEMENTS

14 Hours 'Til Bedtime had a long gestation period, but thanks to the help of many people, its birth was most spectacular. I couldn't have done it without the steadfast support of my agents, Dawn Frederick and Laurie Harper. I owe Nancy Cleary of Wyatt-MacKenzie my deepest gratitude for taking her chances on this first-time author. Many thanks, also, to my editor, Terry Doherty, for her keen eye and great advice. A big thanks to my publicist, Robin Blakely, for her great ideas and hard work, and thanks to Mike Moran for making the book come alive with his fantastic illustrations.

Over the years, many readers helped fine-tune the essays that make up this book. Thanks to everyone who put in their two cents, especially Dee Burke, Helen Dolan, Barb Hagner, Liane Lacoss, Lynn Less, Diane Loughlin, Kim Marsden, Jenna Schnuer, Janet Schrot, Lisa Singer, Michael Singer, Monica Singer, Stephen Singer and Susan Stadeli.

A special thank-you to my babysitters, Nina Marraccoli, Brittany Temple and Kara Temple, who entertained the kids so Mommy could "write silly things." And to my mother-in-law, Maria Singer, for making it possible for me to leave the house, think things up and to get a haircut now and then.

Thanks to "The Ladies," my board of directors who have helped me figure out how I'd write and take care of the kids at the same time: Laura Cirone, Jill Cohen, Joanne Dennison, Kathy Fulton, Ann Haaland, Janet Ryan, Maureen Sanders and Chris Schmieder.

Thanks to MommaSaid.net's fans from around the world who write me nice e-mails when I'm having a bad day. And to the folks at Café Café in Butler, NJ, where I wrote parts of this book in peace and quiet.

Thanks to my parents, Bobbie and Keith (a.k.a. Captain Red Pen) Perkins, who have been my first-line editors since I learned how to write. Thanks also to my brother, Scott Perkins, who thinks he deserves a cut of the profits because he taught me how to read. (You'll get nothing and like it.)

Thank you to my husband, Pete, who continues to encourage me to write, even if it's about him. You are the best coach, cheerleader and fan I've ever had. And finally, to my sons, Nicholas and Christopher, whom this book is about. You are, indeed, the light of my life - even on the days you sit on the couch in your wet bathing suits.

A portion of the proceeds from 14 Hours 'Til Bedtime will

be donated to the Endometriosis Association. I have been a

long-time sufferer of endometriosis, a chronic disease

where the lining of the uterus attaches to other parts of the

pelvis causing pain, fatigue and infertility. After four

laparoscopic surgeries and a partial hysterectomy, I still

suffer from chronic pain. Thank you for helping fund the

research necessary to find a cure. For more information

about endometriosis, visit the Endometriosis Association's

web site: **www.endometriosisassn.org.**

~ **Jen Singer**

INTRODUCTION

Comic Relief for Real-Life Desperate Housewives

"To me, housewife is as appealing a title as septic tank cleaner.
Mention either at a cocktail party, and suddenly no
one wants to stand near you."

In my mother's day, being a stay-at-home mom was practically mandatory. Nowadays though, with so many moms working to make ends meet, staying home with the kids is seen as a privilege. And the privileged shouldn't complain. Then again, the privileged normally don't spend their days scraping peanut butter off the telephone or rescuing the cat from yet another tea party.

So, an entire generation of stay-at-home moms, who grew up when women were suddenly expected to "bring home the bacon and fry it up in a pan," seems to downplay their (unpaid) jobs. Yet they work 14-plus hour days, putting aside their own interests – such as conversing with adults in full sentences – with little recognition. Or sleep.

In *14 Hours 'Til Bedtime: A Stay-at-Home Mom's Life in 27 Funny, Little Stories*, I'll say what other at-home moms have been afraid to say: it's really, really hard to devote all your time to little people who show their appreciation by hanging from your belt loops, whining, while you make macaroni and cheese shaped like SpongeBob SquarePants. Again.

And, just like on my award-winning site, www.mommasaid.net, *the stay-at-home mom's coffee break*™, I'll keep it short. Between each story are Just a Minute! breaks – quick, little funnies you can read while stirring the mac n' cheese. Even the essays are brief, because I know you have only about 750 words to read before someone figures out you're hiding in the bathroom with a book.

Since the first printing of *14 Hours 'Til Bedtime*, numerous moms from around the world have told me that not only did the book give them much needed laughs, it made them feel less alone in their daily struggles to tame kids, diapers and piles of laundry. Hearing from them has been a true privilege for me.

So go ahead. Read a little bit and enjoy. Because you deserve it, Mom!

Jen Singer
January 2005

TABLE OF CONTENTS

PART 5 THE WEE HOURS

PART 1
DAYBREAK

How to Succeed at Motherhood without Really Trying

Shifting from working girl to stay-at-home mom can cause culture shock. Anything you learned in the workplace no longer applies. Or does it?

Transfer: Moving the baby from your right arm to your left.

Downsize: When you finally fit into your pre-pregnancy jeans again.

Floating Holiday: Spending Labor Day in the kiddie pool, trying to keep your kids from drowning each other.

Receptionist: Your four-year-old, who has just discovered the Talk button on your cordless phone.

Excused Absence: Surgery. Or a full body cast. Otherwise, you're pretty much on duty all the time.

Company Picnic: Ice pops and tee-ball in the driveway on a warm Tuesday afternoon.

Performance Review: Annually, in bed, on Mother's Day. You've done a good job when you receive homemade greeting cards, flowers and what appear to be Froot Loops mixed with grapes and chocolate chips.

Equal Opportunity Policy: Everyone is given an equal opportunity to fold the laundry, but you're the only one who ever takes it.

Reception Area: The spot near the door where the kids shower Daddy with hugs and accolades, even though you're the one who just spent eleven hours making new outfits for Barbie, reading *You Can Name 100 Cars* twenty-three times and vacuuming dried Play-Doh from between the couch cushions.

Sick Day: Doing the same thing you do every day, only you feel worse than you normally do.

Company Stationery: Whatever scrap of paper you can find to scribble a note to the teacher on before the bus arrives - usually, the back of a Toys "R" Us receipt.

Layoff: "Would you lay off the Cheese Doodles? I'm making dinner!"

Environmental Protection Compliance: A Diaper Genie and a can of Lysol.

Company Parking: Between the tricycles and the recycling containers.

Multi-Tasking: Emptying the dishwasher, filling sippy cups with apple juice and calling your child in sick (again) to the school nurse - all at the same time.

Overtime: Over time, most stay-at-home moms realize there is no overtime in a job that never ends.

Maternity Leave: The hour or so you get to yourself while the hospital nurses clean, weigh and put that cute little pink or blue hat on your newborn.

9 to 5: A half-day.

And What Do You Do?
Searching for a Better Job Title than Housewife

To me, housewife is as appealing a title as septic tank cleaner. Mention either at a cocktail party, and suddenly no one wants to stand near you. Housewife might satisfy the IRS, because it explains in one word your negative cash flow. But it doesn't describe what I do every day, seven days a week with no sick days, holidays or sometimes even bathroom breaks.

In previous years, my accountant had listed my occupation on my tax return as writer. But between last year's pre-term labor (five weeks on the couch) and colic (four months wishing I could put my wailing baby down and sit on the couch), I barely had the time and energy to write a grocery list, let alone something salable. So, I gave up writing to stay home and care for my two young sons. I didn't choose the title for the job.

I could call myself a domestic engineer, like my sister-in-law did. But if I knew anything about engineering, I'd be able to open and close the playpen without stifling more four-letter words than you hear in an episode of "The Sopranos."

Domestic engineer is far too supercilious a title. Mention it at your husband's office holiday party, and people might ask where you got your degree. After a few eggnogs, you might reply, Episiotomy U. or Postpartum State. The next day at your "office," your responses won't seem as clever - except to your mother, who holds master's degrees from those institutions.

Stay-at-home mom sounds benign enough until you've spent three straight rainy days trapped inside with a two year old who thinks Nancy Reagan coined "Just Say No" for him, and a one year old who chews on shoes - including the pair you're wearing. Then you'd realize that stay-at-home mom is an oxymoron.

A stay-at-home mom stays home only when Dad drags the kids to the Home Depot (thank God) or when the governor declares a State of Emergency. Otherwise, she's at a Moms-and-Tots meeting, the supermarket or the mall, dropping quarter after quarter into the Batmobile ride.

"Full-time mom" is another misnomer, because it implies that working mothers are part-time mothers, and that's just not true. Anyone whose Day-Timer® reads "Marketing report due," "Pediatrician appointment" and "Make 18 cupcakes for preschool party" on the same page is not only working full-time at motherhood, she's working overtime.

Besides, "full-time" doesn't even begin to cover how much time I spend at my job. Most full-time workers put in forty to fifty hours a week. I put that in by Wednesday. In my job, I'm on call around the clock. Add family vacations, where I bring my work with me on a very, very long car ride, and full-time becomes all-the-damn-time.

Homemaker is a quaint title, but inappropriate. I haven't made any homes, though I've seen enough construction videos (thanks to my sons) that I probably could build a decent cabin - or at least a nice shed where I could hide. But really, I'm not making a house so much as I'm trying to keep my toddlers from tearing ours down.

In some ways, homemaker sounds worse than housewife. To me, a homemaker does all the same things as a housewife, but with a warm smile and a meatloaf she whipped up between craft projects and Christmas carols. She certainly doesn't have a toddler throwing a tantrum on the kitchen floor, because she won't let him have animal crackers for dinner. A homemaker? By five o'clock, I'm too exhausted to make dinner, let alone a home.

I wish I could think of a better title for the toughest job I've ever had. But no matter what I come up with, my accountant will likely just put housewife on my tax returns anyway. And the Social Security Administration will keep sending me reports with zeros on it. Perhaps that's just how society values what I do.

But the next time someone asks "And what do you do?" I'll just say that I do what my mother did, and her mother did. I'll say it's such a hard job, my husband wouldn't want to do it and my father wouldn't know how. I'll say my kids are very proud of what I do. And they should know, because they come to work with me every day. And then I'll go chat with the septic tank cleaner.

Hurry, Hurry!

The day before my son Nicholas' sixth birthday party was very, very busy for me. I had to get my other son to pre-school, rush back home and bake a cake so it would be cool enough to ice later, and then find the mayor to get the keys to the firehouse, where we were having the party.

I told a friend, "I have to go! I've got to bake a cake so I can meet the mayor!" She understood. She's a mom, too.

Ho, Ho, Ho It's Magic

The other day, I reached into a tissue box in my living room, and pulled out a red foam ball. I was afraid to reach in again. I didn't want to pull out a rabbit.

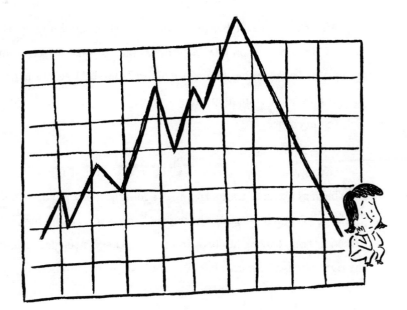

The Great Depression: Pre-Term Labor Ain't for Sissies

Last week, my friend Carol stepped off a Manhattan commuter train and into pre-term labor. Her daughter Meghan couldn't wait until her due date, so she showed up six weeks early. In just twenty-four hours, tiny Meghan staged a hostile takeover that would push her mother into a Great Depression that would remind me of my own.

Though Nicholas rallied from pre-maturity to twenty-four month-size clothes in under a year, I still haven't fully recovered from my postpartum slump. Carol's ordeal brought back the anguish of my own pre-term labor.

All of a sudden, I began crying at baby lotion commercials again. I clung to my son after naptime as though I hadn't seen him for days or weeks, rather than since before "Oprah." I even watched his video monitor at night, putting a Nick at Nite logo in the bottom right-hand corner.

Giving Carol coping advice while in my state of mind would have been as useful as Leona Helmsley running a tax seminar for the "little people." When Carol's hormones kicked in and the hospital kicked her out, leaving her baby in intensive care. I struggled to find the right words to comfort her. All I could do was commiserate.

Like Carol, I went home to a vacant nursery where I tried to capture the magic of mother-newborn bonding with an electronic breast pump that had more in common with a Dustbuster than a baby.

My Great Depression hit me on my last day in the hospital. I call it Black Monday. Nicholas had spent two nights in the Neonatal Intensive Care Unit (NICU). I had spent too much time listening to my hospital roommate's family celebrate her healthy, full-term baby - and whisper about my preemie in the NICU. She had her baby and a roomful of grown men and women who actually believe a hospital curtain holds the same properties as a soundproof wall. I had another five days until I could take my baby home.

When a lactation specialist arrived at my bedside pushing a

bassinet, I thought maybe my baby had had a record-breaking, one-day recovery. I was sure he had miraculously started breathing oxygen without machinery, gained weight and told the doctor he was ready to go home with me.

Instead, she brought me an antique breast pump that looked more like a 1920s ticker tape machine than a lactation device. My roommate nursed her baby and chatted with relatives, while I sat alone, looking like I was awaiting messages from Wall Street about the Crash. By the time my husband arrived to take me home, I was hooked up to the machine, sobbing. He asked if it hurt. It did, but not where he thought. The Crash had arrived.

After we left the hospital, I visited Nicholas as often as possible. I brought vials of breast milk to the NICU to feed him by bottle. He wasn't strong enough to nurse, yet he could chug from a bottle the way a college kid downs a beer. I wondered if he'd be the social chair man of his fraternity someday. I wondered if he'd be out of the hospital and home by then.

When I couldn't stand being home alone without my baby, I went to the party supply store to order birth announcement cards. There, a frazzled mom tried to contain her four-year-old son, who was standing in the shopping cart. "Nicholas! Sit down!" she shouted. I took it as a sign that things would turn out all right.

My Nicholas was finally released from the hospital at seven days old. Though he was just five pounds, nine ounces when he came home, he ranked consistently in the ninety-fifth percentile for length and the seventy-fifth percentile for weight throughout much of his first year - much better than our performance predictions.

He even outgrew one preemie outfit in just two days. Nicholas would chug his way to twenty pounds by his first birthday. And I'd finally get to bond with the baby I hadn't been allowed to hold when he was born.

I assured Carol that Meghan would get home soon and grow as fast as Nicholas did. That soon, she'd wonder how her daughter ever fit into those tiny preemie clothes, so small they look like they belong on dolls, not on children. That soon, she'd be telling her daughter to "Sit down!"

And then I clung to Nicholas like I hadn't seen him since long before *Oprah*.

Holiday

When my friend, Lynn, left for the hospital to give birth to her fourth child, she called it her "four-day vacation." I guess for her, a week in traction at the hospital would be as much a treat as a cruise to the Bahamas.

Road Trip

I read in the newspaper a story about a couple that decided to use maternity leave time for a family trip. As a result, they drove across twenty-five states with a six-week-old baby.

I wonder if they listened to AD/DC's "Highway to Hell" along the way.

It's a Libra! When Baby Wants Out of the Contract Early

Enjoying pregnancy is like finding pleasure in having your kitchen remodeled. Sure, it is fun to plan, and in the end, you get to proudly show off the results to family and friends. But throughout the job, you're just plain uncomfortable and the place is never the same again.

Some women say they "glow" when they're pregnant. The only thing that glowed on my expectant body was the skin on my stomach, because it hadn't seen the sun since before my first positive pregnancy test came back. Put a Home Depot logo on my pregnant belly, and you'd have the kind of glow that announces "Grand Opening" for miles.

I got pregnant the second time when my firstborn was just ten months old. As a result, I got a lot bigger a lot sooner. I felt like a 5,000 square-foot pink stucco house going up in a neighborhood of quaint two-bedroom Cape Cods. By the end of my second trimester, the neighbors started to slow down to check me out in quiet disbelief.

I had lost my curb appeal.

Plus, people didn't make such a big fuss over my second pregnancy as they did with my first. It just wasn't so cute watching me waddle behind my whining, crumb-faced toddler as we rushed through the supermarket aisles.

I was like a store that had kept a "Sorry for the inconvenience while we remodel" sign up a little too long. People began to wonder when it was going to end, and whispered, "Didn't she just do this last year?"

Then one day, my water broke and slowly trickled. I would have been glad that the end was near, except that I was supposed to have more than three months left of my pregnancy. I rushed to the hospital, and prayed for an extension.

In the ultrasound room, the technician showed me my baby's arms, legs, head and heart. She measured him at just over two pounds and twenty-seven weeks gestation - thirteen weeks premature.

I no longer felt my aching feet, nor cared that I couldn't see them over my protruding mid-section. I wanted to be forty weeks pregnant and unable to hoist myself off a sofa. I wanted to be the mother of the biggest baby in the hospital nursery. I wanted to go home pregnant.

While I waited for someone to wheel me back to my room, I watched a clock in the hallway flash the time and date over and over: "1:32 P.M., July 30." My due date was November first. A hospital tech pushed my wheelchair toward the elevator and asked, "What do you want, a boy or a girl?" I answered, "I want a Libra."

After five days in the hospital, I went home to total bed-rest. I had to wake hourly to use the bathroom, because my contractions would start whenever my bladder filled. I kept a portable clock under my pillow that announced each hour in a freakish voice, like one of the munchkins in the *Wizard of Oz*. She'd tell me the hour. I'd go off to see the wizard.

Then, I got some great news. My water had sealed itself over. I wasn't going to have the baby that week. I got my extension.

My doctor told me to limit my activity. He forgot to tell my sixteen-month-old. We were trying to make it to at least thirty-four weeks. When I made it to full-term and then some, I worried that the pregnancy would run late. After three months of bi-weekly ultrasounds and a few false alarms, I felt as though my baby had been hanging around a little too long. I wanted him out.

Finally, nearly three months after I had prayed for an extension, Christopher was born. He was in such a hurry I almost gave birth in the car en route to the hospital. There was no time for an IV. Heck, there was hardly time to remove my clothes. The doctor even showed up after Christopher did.

When I finally held my eight-pound, full-term baby in my arms, I didn't care much that my stomach was bunched up like a collapsible cup with no place to go, or that there hadn't been time for an epidural or even an ice chip to suck on. I was just happy that Christopher was a big, healthy Libra. And that I wasn't pregnant anymore. In fact, that made me so happy that, I swear, I glowed.

Just a Minute!

Dress Up

When Chris was a baby, he was colicky, had reflux and rarely slept more than two hours at a time. I was exhausted and miserable.

Then I saw a TV special about the McCaughy septuplets, and suddenly, I felt better. "At least there aren't seven of him," I'd say over and over to myself at three in the morning, and four in the morning and five in the morning.

Wrong Department

While shopping in the children's section of the bookstore, I spotted a book entitled, *I Don't Want to Take a Nap!*

Obviously, it was shelved in the wrong section. That book belongs in Horror.

The Housewife Awards: A Little Recognition for a Job Well Done

My mother took up tennis for the awards. Now that I'm a housewife, I understand. You don't get trophies for a clean kitchen floor or a plaque because your children say "Thank you," unprompted. My best friend gets plenty of recognition for her work at a pharmaceutical company. She regularly receives bonuses and awards. All I've gotten is the stomach flu and two melted chocolate Easter eggs. And yet, this is the toughest job I've ever had. I've never worked harder.

I used to get flowers on my work anniversary when I was an account coordinator at an ad agency. But at that job, I never had to run down the hall five times a night or mop bodily fluids off the floor. I should have given my boss flowers just for letting me sit down. My current employers - two preschoolers - don't allow it too often.

Somehow my husband can get recognition for doing my job, even if I can't. One day, a neighbor commended him for pushing our kids in the stroller, saying, "Your wife is a lucky woman." For all she knew, Pete had spent 15 minutes pushing the stroller and the rest of the year making a giant ball out of little pieces of aluminum foil. I, on the other hand, am behind that stroller 10 times a day - on Mountain Road. Yes, I am a lucky woman. I now have very nice calves.

At the very least, I deserve Frequent Crier Miles - one mile of air travel for every hour of crying I've endured and consoled. After two babies with colic and 10,000 diaper changes, I'm going to Disney. Euro Disney. Alone.

When my children were born, I should have negotiated a sign-ing bonus - a lump sum of cash just for taking the job. I would have used the money to subcontract out my night shift to someone who can get by on three hours of sleep. My babies never slept through the night, and so neither did I. Aren't there labor laws against excessive-ly long working hours? I ought to sue.

How about a little personal time? For me every day is "Take Our Children to Work Day," minus the media coverage and lunch at a grownup's restaurant. My workday runs from 6 A.M. to 8 P.M. with no breaks, and I'm on call all night, every night. If I had ten minutes to string together, I'd shave both my legs on the same day.

I deserve a Christmas bonus for buying presents for everyone on my family's list, including my in-laws, fourteen pre-school classmates a babysitter who is considering leaving us for a job at McDonald's. I don't want a cash bonus; I just want one Christmas where no one gives my sons gifts that tout "35 Pieces!" on the box, or have "Take Apart" in the title. It'll be a bonus for my vacuum, too.

I'm certain I'd get more job recognition if I worked in, say, fast food. At least I'd get a shot at Employee of the Month, with my photo on the wall. All I've got on the wall now is crayon. If they don't pack a toy in a Happy Meal just right, little will come of it. But if I don't do my job right, it'll cost the neighborhood, the schools and society in the long run.

As a housewife, congratulate yourself for a job well done. You have to find your awards in the look in your son's eyes when he first spots you outside his preschool door. Or in the way your toddler squeals in delight as you race down a playground slide on a sunny Tuesday morning. And yes, even in a clean kitchen floor.

Of course, if you need outside recognition, there's always Mother's Day. Maybe you'll get flowers. Or maybe you'll get some bonus hugs. Or maybe you'll get a few melted Easter eggs and a giant ball of aluminum foil.

Me, I've got my own plan. Tennis, anyone?

Traffic Flow

One day, I had a lot of places to go to. I drove from the pre-school to the kindergarten to the supermarket to soccer practice to my son's friend's house, etc. Each time I went somewhere, I passed over a traffic counter the town had set up to monitor traffic flow on our main street.

If they get a count of 4,000 cars passing by, 3,489 of them will be my mini-van.

Eye Chart

Chris (age five): (from back seat of my car) "Mom? What does this say?"

Me: "I can't read it. I'm driving the car."

Chris: (holding up his magazine) "Here, read it in the mirror."

What am I? A CIA agent?

If You Give a Mom a Cookie

If you give a mom a cookie, she'll ask you for a napkin.

When you give her a napkin, she'll want to wipe her kids' mouths.

Wiping the kids' mouths will remind her that she hasn't packed their school lunches yet. So, she'll ask for the peanut butter.

When you give her the peanut butter, she'll remember she needs to clean that sticky stuff on the refrigerator handle. So, she'll ask for a sponge and some kitchen cleaner.

She'll clean the refrigerator handle, and ask you to hold the door. She'll clean the shelves, the vegetable crisper and the stuff oozing out of the duck sauce jar.

The duck sauce will remind her that she forgot to make dinner reservations for Saturday night. So, she'll ask for the phone.

When she reaches for the phone, it'll ring. So, she'll answer it.

Someone will ask her to volunteer for the upcoming school fundraiser. She'll agree and ask you for a pen and paper. Then she'll hang up.

Hanging up will remind her she forgot to put the dry cleaning away. So she'll go up to her room.

In her room, she'll forget why she went there in the first place. So, she'll go back downstairs.

On the way downstairs, she'll find the phone message about helping with the fund-raiser. She'll pick it up, and ask for the phone.

She'll call a friend, who promises to donate plates to the fund-raiser. The plates will remind her she needs someone to donate napkins. She'll ask you for the napkins.

And chances are, if you give her the napkins, she'll want a cookie to go with them.

Except, someone else already ate it.

PART 2
NAPTIME

Twenty Ways Parenthood is Just Like College

1. You feel like you're constantly being tested.

2. Someone's always smarter than you (or at least they think they are).

3. Your roommates are slobs, and they steal your food.

4. All-nighters.

5. You get kicked out of the library for leaving behind crumbs and creating a ruckus.

6. Keg parties and parties at Chuck E. Cheese produce the same kind of hangover.

7. You never seem to be able to get the place to yourself.

8. Naps.

9. People talk to you while you're in the shower.

10. You hate your roommates' music, and they hate yours.

11. You can neither identify nor locate the source of that funky smell coming from the closet.

12. There's nothing in your bank account.

13. Five in the morning is really, really early - or really, really late - depending on whether or not you've been to bed yet.

14. Hey! How about a pizza? Again!

15. You're too exhausted to retain what you're reading.

16. Oh, now you can identify that smell: You forgot to take that half-eaten sandwich out of the backpack yesterday.

17. You're wearing your college sweatshirt again today, because it's the cleanest thing you could find.

18. Someone always leaves a party crying.

19. You think you're the only one who feels clueless.

20. It goes so fast.

Delta Delta Mom:
The Hazing Begins When You Leave the Hospital

When I was pregnant, I actually thought childbirth was going to be the hardest part about becoming a mother. So when a friend told me, "You're about to enter a special sorority of mothers," I winked at her. I was certain I knew all the sorority secrets: contractions, epidurals, episiotomies. After all, I had read *What to Expect When You're Expecting*. I knew what was coming, right?

But when I went home to care for my baby alone, I realized what my friend had been talking about. The birth is only the initiation into Delta Delta Mom. The hazing begins once you leave the hospital.

Throughout my pregnancy, I had braced myself for what I thought would be the most grueling part of being a new mother - the delivery. Aside from a quick diapering practice on my year-old niece and a glance at a few breast-feeding flyers, I didn't prepare much for the first postpartum weeks.

Turns out, I had braced myself for the wrong thing. For me, Delta Delta Mom's "Hell Week" stretched into a good three months. For much of it, I wasn't allowed to sleep more than two hours at a time. Plus, my son, Nicholas, a preemie, preferred the speed of the bottle to the work of breast-feeding. So I pumped breast milk for weeks, feeling more like a cow on a high-output dairy farm than a new mother.

When a freak spring snowstorm downed the power lines, our electricity shut off whenever I turned the breast pump on. I bundled up my newborn in my bed with me, and reminded him that pioneer babies didn't have electric double breast pumps in the prairie. But he wouldn't take to my engorging breasts, which were beginning to look and feel like the creepy, oozing rocks on "Star Trek."

I realized that although I hadn't changed my pillowcase in quite a while, it was as fresh as the day I had put it on. I had hardly spent time in my own bed. I wish I could say the same thing about the sweatshirt I was wearing.

Nobody had called, but then, what would I talk about anyway?

That my biggest accomplishment for the day was locating the pacifier under the couch? Or that my breasts felt like eggs in a microwave oven? My father, among others, would never have called again. And then I'd really be lonely.

The power came on long enough for me to fix lunch for Nicholas. My breasts let down like a hole in Hoover Dam. Nicholas, meanwhile, filled his diaper so thoroughly, it was as though he didn't want to waste space. How thoughtful.

I wiped and wiped, but I was getting nowhere with that mess. It was like soaking up the Exxon Valdez oil spill with a roll of paper towels. I giggled at the analogy, but Nicholas didn't. All through Hell Week(s), he never laughed, nor even smiled. Most of the time, I didn't either.

I fantasized about following the cat outside to nap in the woodpile. Snow or no snow, it seemed more comfortable than being inside. But the yard might as well have been a day's trip away.

The mailbox seemed so far, I didn't go there for days. Meanwhile, my husband was traveling on business to, I don't know, Chicago or Austin or someplace far beyond the mailbox. To me, it may as well have been the moon. Then I had to get the moon out of my head, because it was even more alluring than the woodpile; no one would be able to find me there.

Hours passed, and then the colic started. It started everyday at dusk, as though the sun sucked all the happiness out of Nicholas as it set behind the hills. He cried. I cried. He cried some more. This went on for hours, while I fantasized about the woodpile (and the moon) the way I used to dream about Spring Break.

In contrast, my labor and delivery room was rather appealing. People plumped my pillow, which I actually used. They fixed my meals. They gave me drugs. Turns out, the part of motherhood that I thought would be the hardest was actually the easiest.

Finally, the phone rang. My best friend, pregnant with her first baby, begged me to tell her the truth about just how horrible childbirth is. I told her, "You're about to enter a special sorority for mothers."

Then I waited for the power to come back on.

Just a Minute!

Time Flies

Back when I got sleep in two-hour increments:

My husband, Pete (*perky*): "Doesn't time seem to be going by quickly?"

Me (*cranky*): "No. Time seems to be going by very, very sloooooowly. Maybe that's because I'm awake for most of it."

Seen on a Billboard: "Dress for the Mess"

I thought someone had finally created a line of stain-proof clothing for mothers of toddlers. Then I realized the construction worker pictured on the billboard was probably not on his way to a "Mommy and Me" class.

Mommy U: Mom's a Child Care Major; Dad Skims Her Notes

When I was little, my mother took up decoupage. It's a perfectly nice hobby, I suppose. Except my mother is not exactly the Martha Stewart type. Her idea of an artist's inventory is a few golf pencils, a pair of thirty-year-old scissors and a crusty bottle of Elmer's glue left over from my history class presentation in 1979. So the image of my mom pasting sketches of furry little field mice onto wooden plaques should be at the very least baffling. Except that now that I'm a mother, I understand.

Mom was what the politically correct call "a primary caregiver." Back then, most people called it "a mother," and, despite the changing tables in the men's room at McDonald's, I call it "a mother," too.

Whatever the semantics, it's the person who is ultimately in charge of the children. It's the one who makes the majority of the decisions regarding whether the kids need a fresh diaper, a pacifier, a snack, a time-out, a sweater, a signed permission slip, a hug, a pair of cleats, a friend, a piano lesson, a training bra, a curfew, a dorm room, a visit. It's the person who sometimes needs to hide from her endless responsibilities in the study and paste scrap paper onto wood.

Since Nicholas was born five months ago, I have become that person. My husband has not. While he's much more helpful with the baby than my father's generation of When-is-dinner dads, he's not in charge.

In fact, if my home were a university, I'd be majoring in Child Care, with a minor in Letting the Cat In and Out. For Pete, Child Care would be an elective course where the little professor praises him just for showing up.

I chose this major when I got pregnant, and I have no regrets. But it is a lot more work than I thought it would be - work that never seems to end. There's no Spring Break at Mommy U., no semester abroad, no playing Frisbee in the Quad between classes with handsome frat boys. Just diapers and spit-up and 2 A.M. feedings.

While Pete's not exactly doing the wave with the university mascot, he's not pulling all-nighters, either. The professor saves those for Child Care majors like me. Pete doesn't have to read thick textbooks that cover everything from "Managing the Symptoms of Colic" to "Respiratory Irregularities" to "When to Call the Doctor." He can get by with skimming my notes; his Child Care course is merely pass/fail. I'm graded on a curve, however, and Sarah Jessica Parker is screwing up the curve.

I have been required to attend long, grueling labs, often in the middle of the night. I've hooked up tubing and vials to my chest, suctioned gunk out of Nicholas' nose and administered a seemingly endless array of semi-effective teething remedies.

In an ongoing lab, I have placed and replaced diapers every few hours, taking note of the contents for a monthly report to the pediatrician. Pete reports the contents to me in a tone of both disgust and wonder, like a tenth grade biology student giving the details of his first frog dissection to the director of the city morgue.

Pete's elective course rarely requires him to attend late night labs. He's been asleep in the Student Lounge during most of mine. I can often hear him snoring from down the hall in the Testing Room. I've tried to get his attention via the Playskool P.A. system that the professor uses to summon me with, but Pete never hears me. Perhaps he failed his freshman hearing test. That probably explains why I rarely see him in my Letting the Cat In and Out class.

After just five months as a Child Care major, I'm tired. But Mommy U requires some eighteen to twenty years to complete a degree. Advanced degrees can take as long as thirty years, especially if the professor gets tenure and won't leave the house.

So, I'm considering taking up decoupage as a "cake course," an easy A. Even if I were to fail, it wouldn't affect my overall grade at Mommy U. Decoupage 101 doesn't carry nearly as many credits as my Child Care major. Besides, Martha Stewart isn't around to screw up the curve.

Just a Minute!

Relax ...

The other night, I finally plopped down on the couch at 9 p.m. I let out a big grunt and said, "I haven't sat all day."

Pete, a computer systems analyst, let out a big grunt, sat down and said, "I sat all day."

Wise guy.

Home, Sweet Home

Nicholas (age four): "Why don't you go to work and Daddy stays home?"

Me: "Because Daddy wouldn't last a day at home."

Daddy: "Try an hour and a half."

More or Less Likely to Succeed:
The Trajectory from High School to High Chair

I think it's time that I stepped down as "Most Likely to Succeed" of my high school class. Why? Because anyone who spends a rainy Friday afternoon during a school holiday week at a crowded children's theme restaurant - the kind with singing stuffed gorillas and greasy pizza - cannot be called a success.

Unlike me, my male cohort in the illustrious title wasn't there that rainy Friday. He was probably cashing in his stock options from some dot-com company, or perhaps visiting his parole officer. Either way, he's doing better than I am.

I'm not sure what my high school classmates expected of me fifteen years ago when they declared me the one girl most likely in our entire class to succeed. I doubt, however, that they pictured me watching helplessly as my three-year-old sank farther and farther into a cage full of bacteria-ridden plastic balls and hyperactive gradeschoolers. Nor do I think they envisioned me plunking dozens of tokens into arcade games, so my sixteen month old could push one button and run away. Most Likely to Succeed? No. Most Likely to Get a Sinus Infection. At least I've accomplished that much.

My classmates probably awarded me the honor because I was president of our senior class. It's an impressive-sounding title; after all, I was president of some 200 people. Now, I'm a co-president of just four people and a cat - and he didn't vote for me.

Of course, when I was senior class president, it didn't matter much if I didn't show up for work. The school functioned just fine without me.

Around here though, things are quite different. When I recently scheduled a minor surgical procedure for myself, I had to consult my husband, in-laws, parents, a baby-sitter and a neighbor to ensure proper babysitting coverage during my absence. It took upwards of nine people to replace me for a day or two, and yet I don't even have an official title or a bake sale to run. President Bush could get a day off more easily, and he gets to retire soon enough. I've still got decades left in office.

Maybe my classmates thought my role as captain of the girls' soccer team might lead to future success. I represented our team in the coin toss, and acted as field liaison to the referee in case, for example, we needed to know how much time was left in the game.

Back then, I had an entire team, a coach, an athletic director and a few fans (parents) to support me. Not anymore. When my husband leaves for work on Monday morning, it's two-on-one: the boys versus Mommy. All I can do is drop back, play a zone defense and hope they don't absolutely clobber me. There are no substitutions in this game, and the other team is relentless. Worse, the game lasts 14 hours - on a good day.

It could have been my role as photography editor of the yearbook that impressed my classmates. I was one of several photographers to capture our senior year on film, so everyone could look back in their thirties and wonder how they could vote for someone who wore leg warmers and a Flock of Seagulls T-shirt as Most Likely to Succeed.

Today, I'm still a photography editor of sorts. It's my job to take pictures of my kids putting toast jam-side-down in their hair, watching *It's Potty Time* from the Elmo potty in the middle of the kitchen, sliding butt-first down the playground slide and trampling the pachysandra. All this, so my kids can look at these photos in thirty years and wonder how in the world they were ever voted Most Likely to Succeed in high school. (Hey, a mom can dream, can't she?)

In the age of corporate multi-millionaires, I'm finding it difficult to measure success by my attendance at a children's birthday party, or how many times I wipe runny noses and teary eyes or if I zipper up little jackets when there's a chill. These may not be the most glamorous responsibilities, but they are among the most important I'll ever have. Doing them right is the greatest success there is. I just have to remind myself of that when I'm yanking my son out of the ball pit at Petey's Pizza.

If my former classmates want to know what their Most Likely to Succeed is doing today, I might tell them about that rainy Friday afternoon. And I might tell them that I'm heading back this Friday with a pocket full of tokens. I'll just leave out the part about the sinus infection. I don't want to brag.

It's Elective

My brother, Scott, called me the day after I'd had elective surgery.

Scott: "Why is it so quiet there?"

Me: "The kids are at my in-laws. I had my surgery yesterday."

Scott: "You'll do anything for a day off."

Mosh Pit

I was at a Chuck E. Cheese birthday party, watching the mechanical animals sing, when suddenly the entire party of pre-schoolers rushed the stage. Soon, kids were dancing with Chuck E. Cheese and jumping off the stage, shouting "Wahooo!"

I believe this is how Ozzy Osborne got started.

Off the Geek Path: *Still* a Freshman at Mommy U

Every time I think I've got my kids all figured out, they change. Suddenly, the good napper won't nap, the good eater wallpapers the restaurant with his pizza, and the most popular toy in the house is not a Tonka truck, but the business reply card from my husband's *Woodworking* magazine. The next day, everyone sleeps, no one eats and that business reply card ends up abandoned in the bathtub.

It makes me feel as though I'm back at college on the "Geek Path," a dirt trail traversed only by unsuspecting freshmen, who were consequently shoved off by upperclassmen. Only, I keep getting back on Mommy U's Geek Path. My kids keep pushing me off.

I've been a mother for nearly three years, and yet, I'm still just a freshman at Mommy U. Half the time, I don't know what I'm doing or where I'm going. The first months were difficult, but it wasn't until after baby number two was born that I started failing test after test. It was like transferring mid-semester from a junior college to Harvard: I'm in over my head.

Caring for two kids under three is like having a pop quiz every few hours on material that's not in the textbook. You just have to take your best guess and pray you don't fail. Still, I flunked math early on. I had thought that one plus one equals two, but not at Mommy U. Here, one nineteen month old plus one newborn equals some exponential number that's too difficult to total on just four hours of sleep. Add colic, and your calculator freezes up.

The multiple-choice questions got harder after I became a mother for the second time. Suddenly, I had to answer: To whom do you tend in this split-second parenting dilemma?

a. the hysterical toddler who is hanging by his overalls from the playground slide;

b. the baby crawling into the path of third graders wrestling over a Pokémon card;

c. the dog who is running away with your diaper bag and therefore, your car keys;

d. all of the above.

The correct answer is d, but you don't learn how to do all of the above until sophomore year. And at this rate, I'm not going to make it there until my kids are answering their own multiple-choice questions - on the SATs.

Chemistry is another subject that got harder after my second child was born. I thought I had devised a simple hypothesis: combining two toddlers with a neighborhood Halloween party would produce a nice afternoon.

But I forgot to factor in the table full of easy-to-reach cupcakes; one poopy diaper trapped under a dragon costume with no snaps; and the properties that attach silver glitter to brand new olive-colored, dry-clean only pants. Heat the entire thing up to about 80 degrees Fahrenheit, and soon, the toddlers exploded into tears. And so did I.

I'm not doing well in journalism, either, because I keep flunking current events. I can't keep track of everything that's going on around me. If, for example, I'm helping my three year old out of the sandbox, I don't notice that my sixteen month old is selecting rocks for a snack. When I answer the phone, it takes me a while to realize that one kid is clearing all twenty-nine videotapes from the cabinet, the other is washing up - in the toilet - and the cat is finishing my cereal. I think I'll pass on the internship at *The Toddler Times*.

With two toddlers in the house, psychology has become my

worst class of all. I can't explain their behavior if I don't understand it. Surely, anyone who likes to hear Elmo sing "Octopus' Garden" three dozen times in a row and demands to have both a toy cement mixer and the vacuum cleaner's attachments in bed with him and can eat rice only if it comes from Daddy's plate, must have some sort of disorder or phobia or something. It just can't be normal.

I'm beginning to figure out that I will always be a freshman at Mommy U. I'll always wander around lost and confused, because my kids will keep changing. But there is one lesson I've learned already: Motherhood is one long Geek Path that spans from the maternity ward to the kids' graduation ceremonies. Like the freshman mothers before me, I'll keep getting pushed off, but I'll keep getting back on. And why not? There's plenty of company on Mommy U's Geek Path and we moms can always share our notes.

Just a Minute!

The Count

Chris (age four): "….21, 22, 23, 24, 25, 26, 27, 28, 29, um, um 21?"

Me: "That's okay, I can't remember thirty, either. That's the year I became a mother."

Teaching Einstein

Nicholas (age five): "Mom? What else is invisible besides air?"

Me: Oh my. I have an opportunity to help cultivate the mind of a budding scientist. What a responsibility. What an important moment in motherhood. "Um … Um … Wonder Woman's airplane?"

Is it Tomorrow? One Mom's Farewell to Her High Standards

Before I had kids, I had a Type A personality. Now, I'm lucky if I can eek out a C-minus. Parenting has drained me so much; I just don't have the energy to keep my standards up. I even managed to flunk my son's parent-teacher conference, because I hadn't taught Nicholas how to use scissors - a skill, his teacher told me, he should have mastered by his third birthday. I should hand out scissors? Not with what goes on in my house. If his teacher only knew.

Whenever I'm out with my kids, people stop to tell me that my hands are full, as if I didn't already know that. It happens at the pharmacy, when Nicholas and his two-year-old brother are re-stocking the cold medicine shelves. At the mall, when they're playing Hide 'N

Seek in the women's dressing rooms. And at my chiropractor's office when they're helping the doctor adjust my back - with their Tonka trucks. My kids are more likely to run with scissors than to cut with them.

After a while, I gave up on my Type A personality, and settled for a nice, solid B. I went to a hypnotherapist, who gave me a stress-reducing cassette tape to listen to after the kids' bedtime. But every time I got to the part about how I am a "master of stress control," Nicholas would appear at my bedside in search of his rubber lizard.

I'd escort him back to his bed and promise, "We'll look for it tomorrow." Yet as soon as I'd restart my tape, he'd reappear to inquire, "Is it tomorrow?"

I've been asking that for four years.

In time, I became content with a C average. One day, I promised my sons they could play with the train set at the toy store after their much-dreaded haircuts. But the train set had been removed. Soon, so were we, when my cranky kids threw tantrums in the middle of the crowded store.

I whisked them to nearby Chuck E. Cheese's, where eventually, they stopped wailing, and disappeared into the ball pit. Sweaty and exhausted, I collected myself by the "Whack-a-Gator" game. Then, I plunked in some tokens and clobbered plastic alligators with a giant foam mallet. I am a master of stress control.

Then, I was struggling for a passing D. One morning, I stepped out of the shower to find my two boys standing between my towel and me. Nicholas looked up and said, "I want to touch those." I answered, "Don't you all," and shooed my sons out of the bathroom. When Nicholas hits puberty, I'm going to need a parenting tutor. And a drink.

The shower incident must have disturbed them, because they stayed awake much of that night - a night we had a houseguest. For hours, I hushed them, plied them with milk, begged them, threatened them and eventually, lugged them downstairs to try to sleep on the couch.

But no one could sleep because our downstairs telephone, which had broken that day, beeped incessantly. Beep. Beep. Beep. Bee-I stormed to the window, threw it open, grabbed the phone and hurled it into the backyard. Lucky for my kids, they don't beep.

Finally on the brink of failure, I attended a Positive Parenting class, a sort of remedial course for parents with their hands full. The teacher assured us that the dozen or so of us who had shown up were not on the bottom rung of our community's parents, but at the top.

Everyone, he said, has a hard time with "the toughest job on earth," but only a few are willing to admit it. He didn't say how many throw their appliances out the window at four in the morning, but just knowing there might be others made me feel better. Suddenly, I no longer felt like a failure.

Nicholas now knows how to use scissors. I hope his teacher is satisfied. In fact, he's so adept at cutting, he makes fringed placemats for me; I have sixteen so far.

His brother hasn't yet learned to cut with scissors. Instead, he dips them into his cereal bowl and drips the milk all over my placemats. Nicholas gets angry, and sets out to make more from whatever paper he can find, including, so far, my crossword puzzle, the mortgage bill and the "Where Will You Be in the Year 2000?" section of my high school yearbook.

Is it tomorrow?

Ladies Night?

At a parenting seminar last year, one woman lamented that her husband would treat her time there as a night off, as though "Disciplining without Yelling" could be anything like a ladies' night at the movies or dinner out with friends.

"Tell him it's a work-related seminar," I offered. "And that you deserve a raise."

Shopping Lists

When Nicholas was a colicky baby, I was deliriously tired. When my husband told me to bring home Parmesan cheese from the supermarket, I did. And I did the next time, too. And the next. By the time Nicholas was three months old, we had eight containers of Parmesan cheese.

When our Christopher was a colicky baby, I brought home seven jars of chili powder over a six-week period. We're not having a third baby. Our kitchen doesn't have room.

**Mommy Doesn't Always Know Best:
Kindergarten Readiness for Dummies**

I'm supposed to be the one who knows what's best for my children. After all, I'm the Mommy. Plenty of people told me so when I had to decide whether Nicholas would go to kindergarten or to junior kindergarten, a program in our public school for kids who need extra time to prepare for our highly academic (and highly rated) school system. But I found out later, maybe Mommy doesn't always know best. Sometimes, the teachers do.

When I received the letter from the public school that recommended Nicholas for junior kindergarten, I wasn't surprised. My gut told me he needed a little more time to mature enough for a school system where the second graders write book reports about famous people and the kindergarteners count pennies, nickels and dimes. So, basically, seven year olds write biographies and five year olds practice accounting. My son could wait.

Though he was five, he had tested between ages four-and-a-half and five on the kindergarten readiness test, while the "kids who do best in kindergarten," as I was told, test between five and five-and-a-half. Geez. When I was a kid, the kindergarten readiness test went like this:

"Are you five?"
"Yeah."
"You're ready."

Not anymore.

"But he's so smart!" my mother-in-law protested. Surely a five-year-old who wanted to know how clouds stay up in the sky and why tires are black belongs in kindergarten, right?

But, I explained, this isn't about smarts; it's about maturity. In our school system, kindergarteners don't play "Ring Around the Rosie" and make flowers out of tissue paper like we did. Today's kindergarteners add. They read. They discuss long and short vowels. They contemplate the Big Bang Theory. Okay, not the Big Bang

Theory, but they do things I didn't do until second grade. And Nicholas wasn't ready.

Yet over the summer, he grew up quite a bit. He started drawing, proof to me that his "immature" fine motor skills had grown up, too.

One August night, he appeared in our living room two hours after his bedtime, carrying an 11x17-inch piece of paper. He had drawn an elaborate dinosaur scene, complete with erupting volcanoes and battling pterodactyls. This from a kid who that June, could barely press down hard enough to write his name.

He sighed. "I'm really tired, but I just want to color!"

I replied, "Who are you, and what have you done with my son?"

In the days that followed, Nicholas changed so dramatically, I was certain he was ready for kindergarten. He became more self-confident. He accepted "no" for an answer instead of collapsing into a heaving ball of misery on the floor. And he colored constantly, even when he was really tired.

So on the first day of school, I called the principal to tell her I wanted to put Nicholas in kindergarten. To her credit, she didn't dismiss me as a lunatic mother. Instead, she and the junior kindergarten teacher observed Nicholas in school, she let me observe a kindergarten class and she set up a meeting to reveal the verdict: my son belonged in junior kindergarten.

I was certain they had an alternate agenda. Maybe there was a quota to fill. Maybe they didn't want their readiness tests proven wrong. Maybe they thought I was a lunatic mother. So I made them put him in kindergarten for a week. After all, I know my son best. I'm his mother.

Nicholas tried hard in kindergarten, and I tried hard with him. We spent lots of time on his homework together. We spent lots of time talking about how much fun he was having there. We spent lots of time trying to pretend this would work out fine.

But that Thursday afternoon, I met with the principal and the kindergarten teacher, and it all became clear: he just wasn't where the other kids were in class. He needed more time.

That night, I called a child psychologist friend to ask how I can explain to my son why he'd have to go back to junior kindergarten. I didn't want him to feel like a failure. And I didn't want to feel like a jerk, although I did.

I prepared to tell him that weekend, but Friday morning he announced, "I want to go to junior kindergarten." I told him that his teacher had called and said she and his classmates missed him. He'd go back on Monday, but that day, we'd play hooky.

I'm glad the teachers proved me wrong. Or was it Nicholas who proved me wrong? He's grown up so much in junior kindergarten, I'm certain he's more than ready for kindergarten. He's more mature, and as smart as ever. He even asked me to explain the Big Bang Theory. I told him, "You'll learn that in first grade."

Just a Minute!

A Few of My Favorite Things

My son's junior kindergarten class had a class trip to go maple sug-aring at a nearby park. The kids and parents all filed into a shack and took their seats among posters of maple trees and bottles of maple syrup. The park's instructor introduced herself and said, "Now boys and girls, we're going to learn about something I really love to do. What do you think that something is?"

A little girl replied, "Shopping!"

Cleaning Service

One of Nicholas' five-year-old friends was in my car for the first time. As I strapped him in his car seat, he looked at the car floor and said, "You know, you could clean this up."

I was about to say, "You know, I could take you home." But he was busy offering me his grandfather's Shop Vac®. Apparently, it would take an industrial strength vacuum to clean up that mess.

Introduction to the Toddler Curriculum

Math: Students will learn the relationships of points and angles, particularly with respect to coffee table corners at forehead level. They will learn that a toddler leaving the living room at five miles per hour will arrive at the top of the basement stairs later than a mommy leaving the kitchen at one hundred miles per hour, no matter how many times they try it.

Science: This course will teach students cause and effect. Students will learn that repeatedly racing around the kitchen table in their socks singing "Baby, baby, dip your nose in gravy" while Mommy is on the phone with the bank loan manager, will land them on the couch for a viewing of *There Goes a Boat* and their mommies in the medicine cabinet in search of Tylenol.

Social Studies: Students will learn about cultures foreign to them, including those where dropping mashed potatoes onto the floor is frowned upon. They'll discover that not everyone finds flushing and re-flushing the toilet an entertaining activity. And they'll find out that other groups of people actually prefer sleeping at 2 A.M., rather than singing the theme from "Elmo's World" into the baby monitor.

English: This class introduces English to children who say, "Goo," when they mean, "I want to chew on your shirt buttons." Students will learn such useful English terms as "Uh oh," "sippy cup" and

"No!" Advanced students will learn to say "Mama" before "Dada," if they know what's good for them.

Art: This course will introduce students to the classics - Winnie the Pooh, Clifford, Big Bird - as represented in crayon, Play-Doh and/or ketchup-on-high chair. Advanced students will learn to create a sizable mural with "Blues Clues" toothpaste and a bar of soap.

Home Economics: Students will learn about the art of home management and how to make it extremely difficult for their parents to perform it. By the end of the course, students will be able place the contents of the toy box in the dishwasher, the contents of the dishwasher in the bathtub and the bath toys in Daddy's briefcase.

Health: Students will learn how the body functions, and then promptly forget about it when Mommy mentions using the potty. Considerable time will be spent discussing the left and right nostrils, especially when there are peas for dinner.

Physical Education: Students will hone their athletic skills, particularly when the nurse at the pediatrician's office pulls out a syringe. Other athletic activities include: holding marathon crying fits at bedtime; running naked and wet from the bathtub; and repeatedly kicking the seat in front of them at church.

PART 3
THE WITCHING HOUR

Mommy Milestones

The first year of a child's life is filled with milestones. So, too, is the first year of motherhood.

Birth to One Month

• Sees her own feet for the first time since coming home from the twenty-week ultrasound.

• Figures out how to put the infant car seat into the car in forty-three minutes.

One to Three Months

• Holds her own head up, at least long enough to see the teetering pile of baby-shower thank-you notes that have yet to be written.

• Smiles (especially when someone else cooks dinner).

• Uses baby talk, even with mother-in-law and when ordering Chinese food by phone.

• Stops calling the expiration dates on milk and other refrigerated food items "due dates."

Three to Six Months

• Sleeps through the night.

• Laughs.

• Buttons pants.

• Figures out how to put the infant car seat into the car in twenty-seven minutes.

Six to Nine Months

• Eats solid food (filet mignon with béarnaise sauce) ... Thanks for babysitting, Grandma!

• Crawls - through a pile of baby toys that squeak and sing - in the dead of night to find the pacifier that the baby threw out of the crib.

• Swears to pick up the pile of baby toys first thing in the morning.

• Remembers the pile only as she trips over it in the afternoon while carrying a load of laundry.

• Apologizes to own mother for every rotten thing she did as a kid, because she finally understands.

• Figures out how to put the infant car seat into the car in six minutes.

Nine Months to One Year

• Walks - with the stroller, up and down hills, in the rain, the cold and the sweltering heat - because it's the only way a certain some-one ever takes a nap anymore.

• Talks to husband for several minutes without an interruption.

• Figures out how to put the infant car seat into the car in ninety seconds while opening a box of animal crackers-then discovers she has to buy a new car seat because the baby's too big.

• Bakes a very special "You're 1!" birthday cake, only to watch baby put two grubby little hands into the carefully constructed roses.

• Wonders where the year went.

Just a Minute!

Because I Love You

When I was pregnant with my first son, I wore a big, purple maternity dress to a family gathering.

After waddling behind my then fifteen-month-old niece around the table a few times, I asked my family, "Do I look like Barney in drag?"

Sweets for Mommy

Me: "What'd you do in school today?"

Chris: "We made cookies."

Me: "For the Mother's Day party?"

Chris: "Yeah."

Me: "Will I get one?"

Chris: "If you behave."

Me: "I'll try."

Overtime: When Family Planning Takes Longer Than Planned

My high school sex education class made getting pregnant seem oo easy. A family planning filmstrip showed my classmates and me just how easy. All you need is a team of sperm to skate through the womb until one reproductive teammate gets close enough to take a shot on goal - the egg. The key to preventing pregnancy, the film said, was a strong defense.

But I didn't discover until I was nearly thirty that trying to get pregnant can take a whole lot more than pulling your goalie out of the net. In fact, it's a different ballgame altogether.

By the time Pete and I were ready to play the reproduction

game, I thought I could simply stop using birth control and plan my baby's delivery for nine months later, as if I were penciling a Rangers vs. Flyers game into my schedule.

I've since learned, however, that it works that way only for people who don't want to get pregnant. For the rest of us, there's far more work involved.

When Pete and I decided to become parents, we didn't anticipate any reproduction game delays. At twenty-eight, I thought there was plenty of time left on my biological clock - until I turned twenty-nine and my copy of *What to Expect When You're Expecting* was being used as a coaster.

I had bought the wrong playbook. A health manual I later found revealed that it takes women in their late twenties an average nine months to conceive. Nine months? My high school sex education filmstrip had used the wrong sports analogy. This was no hockey game. It was the Iditarod, or perhaps an Iron Man competition. Just ask my husband.

When we didn't get onto the scoreboard right away, my obstetrician suggested that I chart my body's temperature to help determine when I was ovulating. I woke up every morning at 6:45, placed a thermometer in my mouth and promptly fell back asleep.

I soon splurged on state-of-the-art equipment - a $70 ear

thermometer. In time, I created something that looked more like a football team's playbook than an ovulation chart. It didn't help me determine my most fertile days, but it did give me great tips on punting on fourth down.

The constant shift in the length of my menstrual cycles from twenty-eight days up to as long as thirty-five days made things even more confusing. But I still ripped open a home pregnancy test whenever I reached the thirty-third day in a futile Hail Mary kind of play. Month after month, I never saw the "pink for positive" sign I longed for. After a while I felt like the Boston Red Sox. Not a championship in sight.

I gave up on my ovulation charts when one doctor declared them "not encouraging," and another said they "looked good." (I considered sending my charts to the NFL, but I tucked them into my *Expecting* book instead).

One month, my doctor prescribed a low dose of fertility drugs designed to help stimulate ovulation. My insurance company wouldn't cover the $60 cost for the five pills, but I imagined that was a politically correct decision. After all, they hadn't covered the pills that prevented ovulation, either.

Yet I guessed they would have picked up the tab if my husband had needed a prescription to help make his sperm move faster. They probably would have run a special promotion called "Swim to Win," providing each new patient with a free sports towel and swim goggles. All I got, though, were hot flashes.

On those pills, I felt I wasn't on the verge of motherhood, but menopause. I went from imagining myself in a maternity dress to picturing myself in front of a giant air conditioning vent. I had more in common with grandmothers than mothers, and I hadn't even hit thirty yet. Maybe, I thought, I should just retire my number and go play golf.

Then one cycle, on the thirty-third day, I discovered that we were finally winners in what had pretty much become the Sex Olympics. That night, I told Pete we were going to Disney World (in a few years, anyway). I expected a hug, or at least a high five. But he just laid down on the floor, panting, as though he had just crossed the finish line at a marathon.

In the end, I decided that my high school sex education class filmstrips were right to use a hockey analogy to explain conception. I wish only that they had warned me about overtime.

Baby Sleeps Through Night!
When "Sleeping Like a Baby" is a Bad Thing

Here's a headline worthy of a supermarket tabloid: "Baby Sleeps Through the Night." I'd sooner believe "Elvis Predicts the World to End Thursday After *The Apprentice*." My son Nicholas has never slept through the night. Yet it seems everyone I know has told me unbelievable stories about babies who do. I try not to nod off when someone starts yet another tale about a baby who doesn't keep raccoon's hours. But I haven't had a full night's sleep since before Nicholas was born, and I need to nap whenever I get the chance.

At a recent picnic, the mother of a baby just three days younger than Nicholas claimed her child never had any sleep difficulties. "Sarah's been sleeping through the night since the beginning," she offered in that perky way only people who have achieved REM sleep can muster. I wanted to peg her in the head with my hot dog, but I was too tired to lift my head above the horizon, let alone throw a curve ball. Besides, Sarah was napping in her arms. Naturally,

Even Nicholas' doctor believes babies sleep. Before I left the hospital, he had instructed me to feed my newborn every four hours, even if that meant waking him up. On the third night of on-demand feeding sessions every sixty to ninety minutes, I considered waking the doctor up. I wanted to ask him what the heck he had been talking about.

In his third week, Nicholas developed colic. Even if he had wanted to sleep, his turbulent tummy wouldn't let him - or me. I spent hours, day and night, rubbing his belly and trying to aim baby gas relief drops into his mouth between sobs - his and mine.

Soon, the only way I could tell the difference between three in the afternoon and three in the morning was that in the wee hours of dawn, the sky was dark and my husband snored. Hey! Maybe I was supposed to wake him up every four hours.

For a while, I hung onto the idea that the tales about babies who miraculously started sleeping through the night at just three months old were true. Then Nicholas turned three months old, and I wondered, at one 2 a.m. feeding, if in my sleep-deprived haze I had heard three months when it was really three years. It sure felt like three years.

When Nicholas finally outgrew his colic, I put away his gas relief drops and imagined I'd soon be telling people about the first night my baby didn't wake me up. I ran my fingers over the "Sleeps Through Night" sticker in his baby milestone book, and daydreamed about putting it on the calendar.

Within a few days, I had used the "Rolls Over," "Eats Cereal and Laughs" stickers, leaving "Sleeps Through Night" all alone at the top of the page. If I had a mommy milestone book, the "Laughs" sticker would be keeping "Sleeps Through Night" company.

And so, every night, those irritating words echoed through my head: "Sarah's been sleeping through the night since the beginning." I fantasized about calling Sarah's mom in the middle of the night to give her a run-down of the nocturnal animals foraging through my recycling bins. Instead, I warmed up my throwing arm for the next picnic.

Before I became a mother, I imagined teaching my child to talk, walk and use the potty. But I never thought I'd have to teach him how to sleep. I remember I used to be very good at sleeping; it was one of my favorite things to do. I don't remember ever having to consult a reference book on how to do it.

Until now.

Armed with Dr. Richard Ferber's book, *Solving Your Child's*

Sleep Problems, and the intense desire to remain prone for more than a few hours at night, I "Ferberized" Nicholas. In other words, I let him cry it out. And I cried with him, on the other side of his door. It took a few hours a night for about a week, but finally, at ten months old, Nicholas slept through the night. And so did I. I wore the "Sleeps Through Night" sticker from his baby milestone book like a badge the next day.

Recently, a friend told me she had "slept like a baby" the night before. "Oh, I'm so sorry!" I offered. She looked puzzled. "Let me guess," I said. "You've slept through the night since the beginning."

It's amazing what a little sleep can do for your throwing arm.

Just a Minute!

Sit Down

My cousin's daughter, Kristin, fifteen months old, has little interest in walking. In fact, I watched her sit quietly in her mother's lap on Christmas night for twenty whole minutes, considerably longer than my two boys sat for all of 1999.

When my boys were toddlers, I spent Christmas repeatedly chasing after them up and down the stairs and pulling Christmas ornaments from their mouths. My cousin, on the other hand, spent the holiday chit-chatting about wine.

So, I gave Kristin a Sit n' Spin for Christmas. If she's gonna sit, she oughta spin. I even got the one with music and lights so my cousin can learn how annoying parenthood can be. Clearly, he has no idea.

Napless in New Jersey

One afternoon at the lake, I saw a boy, around two-and-a-half years old, fussing and whining at the edge of the water. For a brief moment, I thought his shirt read "Napless." But then I realized it said, "Naples, FL."

I think "Napless" better summed up his mood.

Colic - 2, Mom - 0: Mom Loses Again

Obviously, there's been a mistake. A recent study claimed that colic has no long-term effects on either baby or mother. Yeah? Then how come even though it's been four years since my youngest outgrew colic, the sound of a newborn wailing *still* makes me break out in a sweat and subconsciously pat-pat-pat whatever I'm holding?

While an average of one in five babies suffers from colic, both my sons had it. Combined, their colic lasted seven months. That's longer than it takes the average hiker to walk all two thousand - plus miles of the Appalachian Trail, only more exhausting. So when someone tries to tell me that I'll forget all about colic - the way, I suppose, I'll forget about natural childbirth - I can't disagree more.

The first time I faced colic, Nicholas fussed and fussed and fussed for an hour or two, but I couldn't calm him down. I tried breast milk. I tried a pacifier. I tried rocking him and singing (okay, sobbing) "You Are My Sunshine," while wishing my husband wasn't on a business trip.

I considered calling my mother in the middle of the night. And then I realized, "I can't call my mommy. I *am* the mommy!"

For three months, I held Nicholas' belly to mine every night, and patted his back repeatedly until finally, about four hours later, he'd fall asleep in my arms on the couch.

A friend asked if I was enjoying this magical time of bonding with my baby. I told her there was nothing magical about it, except perhaps that the second floor of our house seemed to disappear every night. I didn't see it.

So when my younger son Christopher started fussing the day he came home from the hospital, I knew what was coming - three to four months of eating, walking and even dressing while pat-pat-patting my newborn's back for hours at a time.

Chris, who also had acid reflux to aggravate his already aggravated digestive system, fussed from about four o'clock in the morning until 10 A.M., and then again from 4 P.M. until the 10 o'clock news came on at night.

Every day between Halloween and Valentine's Day, people launched new companies, planned weddings, wrote books or, perhaps, painted murals. Not me. All I accomplished was repetitive strain disorder.

Well, it was every day except one. On Thanksgiving, Chris slept quietly throughout dinner, while my family told me, "There's nothing wrong with that baby." I uncurled my arms enough to shove turkey down my throat, and asked, "Can we have Thanksgiving dinner every day?"

One day, I marveled that his colicky bouts were getting shorter. I was spending "only" six hours a day patting his back. Then I realized that six hours a day is forty-two hours a week - longer than the average job, only without the water cooler chitchat about the latest episode of "The Bachelorette."

After a while, I became a bit like Pavlov's dog. At the first sound of any fussing, I'd jump up and start patting my son's back, even if what he needed was a diaper change or lunch. But no one patted my back.

Most people saw Chris between his daily colicky bouts. So, many were skeptical when I talked about it. They told me about how their babies were fussy, too: "She even cried for forty-five minutes last night!"

Amateur.

I started to think I just couldn't handle being a mother. If I could, I'd be sleeping soundly in my bed, instead of dozing upright on the couch, baby in my arms, startling myself awake at his every noise, like a character in a horror film.

Then one day, I returned from a much-needed morning off to find my mother-in-law holding a fussy Chris, his face still red from crying. "He's a miserable baby," she confessed. "He cried all morning, but I couldn't calm him down."

I felt like the first person to spot Sasquatch. Finally, someone other than my husband believed me! I was vindicated. And in a few weeks, it was over. But not forgotten.

Two years later, my next-door neighbor gave birth to a baby boy. Late one night, she called me and shouted into the phone over her newborn's cries, "Come over here RIGHT NOW and tell me if this baby has colic!"

But I didn't have to go next door. I was already pat-pat-patting the phone.

Just a Minute!

Hibernation

Last week, I turned on the radio in the middle of an informational segment. The announcer said: "His breathing and heart rate slow considerably, and he can't hear any noises around him." I thought they were talking about fathers sleeping at night, but it was about hibernating bears.

Call Me

When Chris was a baby who didn't sleep much at all, I warned my child-free college pals not to call me late at night when they all got together for a reunion in Los Angeles.

Sure enough, they called me at midnight my time, waking Pete and me up. I could hear my friends laughing and asking Pete to put me on the phone. I told him to hang up. They called back, but we let our voicemail pick it up.

When my sons got me up at 5:45 the next morning, I listened to my voicemail. "Call us back!" my friends shouted, laughing that "We don't have children. We can sleep whenever we want" laugh.

So, I waited an hour - until it was nearly 4 A.M. in LA - and I called them back.

Funny, they haven't called after 9 P.M. since.

Leaving Mommy Boot Camp: A Little Liberty - at Last

My friend Helen wants to learn how to mow the lawn. She figures it's the only way she can get an entire hour to herself. She's actually jealous of her husband when he pushes the lawnmower around the yard in the blazing heat, because she's stuck inside wiping her newborn's spit-up off the couch for the umpteenth time in a week. Helen is in Mommy Boot Camp. Somehow, so am I, even though I should have graduated months ago.

When your biggest aspiration is to pry your eyes open enough to put in your contact lenses, you're in Mommy Boot Camp. You can only dream of such luxuries as watching entire rental movies and wearing shirts without strained peas ground into the collar. Mommy Boot Camp is for your own good, and for your baby's good, because all your attention is focused on your little bundle of joy (and his big bundles of laundry).

But after three years and two children, I've had enough of Mommy Boot Camp. I'm ready for some small liberties. I long for the chance to sleep while everyone else in the house is awake. I want to put something in the wastepaper basket, and have it stay there. I want to move on, but there's no ceremony to mark the end of Mommy Boot Camp. None, except perhaps the champagne celebration that some moms hold at the school bus stop in September. And I'm a long way from that.

Before Mommy Boot Camp, I fretted over whether the napkins at my wedding reception should match the bridesmaids' dresses. Now I'm ecstatic if there are napkins on the table at all, instead of stuffed into numerous shoes and toy trucks throughout the house. Mommy Boot Camp builds character, and frequently, a tension headache.

Yet while I'm searching toy backhoes for something to wipe my mouth on, other moms have moved on. On the playground recently, a woman read her newspaper while her four year old played independently on the slide. I, on the other hand, tried to stop my three year old from terrorizing the toddlers on the merry go-round while I raced into the woods after my nineteen month old.

The other mom was checking out her horoscope. I was finding

out how fast I can run backwards while yelling. Marines are doing the same thing on Parris Island, only they leave after six weeks. I'm still here.

Yes, I've had some time to myself - two whole days following a minor surgical procedure. The kids went to my in-laws, and I got to rest. I was so excited about spending two days on the couch with the cat you'd think I was going to the beach for two weeks with Matt Damon.

After forty-eight hours of snoozing on and off, I was overwhelmed by the kids' return, much like the Germans on D-Day. The cat retreated. I was cornered in the kitchen. I held up my bag of Cheetos in lieu of a white flag.

Soon, it was back to the grueling fourteen-hour days that begin pre-dawn with "Reveille," sung by my younger son, and end with "Taps," played reluctantly by my older son when he runs out of requests for water, potty visits and reassurance that I'm still on duty.

In between, there are combat maneuvers: I mop the stairwell, while my little one throws toys and dirty clothes from above at my head. It's shrapnel, toddler-style.

While I've been in Mommy Boot Camp, other mothers have graduated shortly after their babies started to sleep through the night. (Mine still don't.) Or when their little ones began sitting in one place longer than even Grandpa does. (Mine never have.) Or when they put something in the garbage can, and it actually stayed there. (Mine, well, you know.)

I started to think something was wrong with me. Maybe I wasn't fit to graduate. Then I realized: I'm in an elite group of mothers with special, long training. I'm with the mothers of triplets and the moms with children who put stink bombs in the mailbox. I'm among the moms of those kids who scream through the super-market and paint their little sisters. In other words, I'm in the Green Berets of moms.

After all, I don't have time to check my horoscope. That's for civilians. I've got to stay vigilant, stay awake and stay in Mommy Boot Camp for a lot longer than I had planned. And that's okay, because at least I don't long to mow the lawn. Well, not anymore.

Just a Minute!

From the Shores of Montezuma ...

On a crowded beach last summer, I ran toward the Port-a-Johns, carrying both my sons, who had left their sandals back at the towels several hundred yards of burning, hot sand behind us. As I raced while lugging eighty pounds in my arms, I thought, Somewhere on a beach in Kuwait or Cuba, there's a Marine doing the same thing. Only not in flip-flops and a tankini.

Fish Story

My doctor had told me to "take it easy" after my surgery.

But one afternoon, Chris and his friend Ryan, both age five, came down into my basement office and asked, "What do you do when the fish falled out of his tank?"

I ran to grab the fish out of his hands and raced up two flights of stairs to put it back in the tank, when I noticed the fish wasn't moving.

"When did he 'falled' out of the tank?" I asked my son.

"Musta been last night," he answered. "Another fish pushed him out."

And so, after my two-flight sprint and a burial at sea, I "took it easy." Yeah, right.

Getting On in Years: When Your Thirties Feel Like Seventy

I think my kids are trying to kill me by aging me rapidly. I was thirty when Nicholas was born three years ago, and now I'm about seventy. At least I feel seventy. In the past year, I threw my back out twice, my cholesterol soared forty-two points and I started tuning my car radio to easy-listening stations. At this rate, I'll be visiting the senior center with my eight-nine-year-old grandmother before I'm forty. I hope I can keep up.

One afternoon, I was lying on the ground, exhausted, when I found proof on TV that my kids are aging me. The author of a book about risk factors for aging said that stress can add up to thirty-two years to your current age. He also said that stay-at-home moms have one of the highest mortality rates among women. That means that I'm eligible for the senior citizen discount at movie theaters, but I'd better hurry if I want to cash in.

Perhaps it's my own fault for spacing my children's births so closely. After having two babies in nineteen months, I felt like Broadway the day after Thanksgiving - the parade had passed through, leaving behind a big mess. I had expected to feel run down for a while, but I never thought I'd feel so old. My kids, however, seem to have planned it from the beginning.

One son was premature; the other tried to be. One spent a week in the Neonatal Intensive Care Unit; the other nearly spent his first minutes in the car en route to the hospital. Both had colic for a combined total of seven months - about as long as two college semesters, but without the keg parties or any measurable fun. One had reflux, a painful digestive disorder that made him (and me) very cranky for ten months; and neither slept through the night before his first birthday. In three years, I had a total of some eight hundred fifty nights - mostly consecutive - of interrupted sleep. Did I say I felt seventy? I meant one hundred.

I thought I'd start feeling younger once we got through the baby years and beyond. But then Nicholas started his "Tyrannical Threes" - his mood ruled the house. His whining, tantrums and tormenting his little brother made "Terrible Twos" seem like the warm-up band for the main show. And I felt like a parent escorting some pre-teens to a Hilary Duff concert: if only it would end, so I could take some Tylcnol and a nap.

So I tried a behavior modification program called "The Smiley Face System." For each of Nicholas' misbehaviors, I crossed out a smiley face on a piece of paper, taking away a treat for every three crossed-out smileys.

On the first day, I had to cross out only one smiley face. I bragged to all my friends, and promised to share the Holy Grail of discipline with them. By nine the next morning, however, Nicholas had lost all his smiley faces. And so had I.

Just when I really needed a break, my Monday afternoon babysitter, Nina, left me for her school's track team. Ahead of me were three months of long Mondays with no Nina. That's when seventeen-month-old Christopher chose his seventh word - Nina. It was actually a string of Nina's, "NinaNinaNinaNina," which I said along with him - between sobs - while crossing out smiley faces. Is it morally wrong to root against your town's high school track team? I just can't afford weeks of championships.

I sought refuge in the bathroom, but my kids wouldn't allow it. I had to hold the toilet seat down with my foot to keep Chris out of the water, while I freed the unraveling toilet paper roll from Nicholas' hands. Then I fielded more of his incessant questions: "Why is Daddy at work?" … "Why don't you work, Mommy?" I told him no one would hire me because I was well past retirement age. Then I returned to my hobby of stopping Chris from repeatedly flushing the toilet.

Nowadays, though, things are improving, however slowly. I get to sleep through the night most of the time, and everyone's tummies usually feel fine. We rarely go through all of Nicholas' smiley faces in one day, and I frequently still have some of mine left at bedtime. Chris has stopped paying homage to his baby-sitter, adding new words every day. Everything was fine, in fact, until he said his seventeenth word, "baby."

Baby? I'm too old.

Jen Singer

Seven Ways to Get Your Kids to Talk To You

Recently I read a pamphlet entitled, "How to Get Your Teenager to Talk to You." I don't know how to get teenagers to talk to you, but I certainly know how to get kids between ages two and six to talk to you:

1. Make a phone call, preferably long distance.

2. Step into the bathroom. Close the door. Lock it.

3. Use a loud appliance, such as a vacuum, hairdryer or blender.

4. Read.

5. Close your eyes for longer than a blink.

6. Try to sneak a cookie before dinner.

7. Make a speech in front of a group of adults that don't get to hear the word "potty" much.

PART 4
BATH TIME

Feng Shui for Toddlers

When I read a recent article about feng shui, the Chinese practice of reconfiguring an environment to harmonize your life, I had to laugh. In my house, two little boys have been reconfiguring my environment their own way.

Feng Shui for Grown-Ups	Feng Shui for Toddlers
Bring the natural world indoors by playing a CD of a rolling surf.	Bring the natural world indoors by opening the sliding glass door and leaving a trail of animal crackers that leads into the kitchen.
Turn off the ceiling lights and use just diffused lights from lamps.	Turn off the bathroom light while Daddy is taking a shower.
Paint a room light blue.	Scribble the living room walls in light blue.
Achieve a "yin" state - a subdued, relaxed feeling - by placing a peaceful painting on the wall near your bed.	Achieve a "yang" state - or chaos - by jumping on the bed.
Sleep on a pastel colored pillowcase.	Sleep on Mommy's pastel-colored pillowcase, and push her closer and closer to the edge of the bed throughout the night.
Add a fountain to your home for a peaceful background noise.	Add Mommy's cell phone to the fountain for a faint ringing noise that Mommy can't seem to locate.
Put a muted fabric over a glass table.	Pour Kool Aid over a glass table.
Create tranquility by putting potted plants in curved patterns along the floor.	Create hostility by placing your Cheerios in curved patterns along the floor.
Drape a blue blanket over a chair.	Drape your blue blankie over the cat.
Toss a muted-colored blanket over a brightly colored bedspread.	Toss your Rockin' Elmo, 17 Legos, your half-full sippy cup and some baby wipes onto a brightly colored bedspread.

In Good Times and Bad Behavior: Do You Still Love Me, Baby?

The day after Nicholas turned one, he turned on me. The same helpless baby who had cooed at me adoringly from his playpen suddenly became a toddler with an attitude. One day, he was hugging me. The next, he was throwing himself toward the floor, pausing briefly to bite me on the way. As I stood there dumbstruck, holding my injured shoulder, I could think only one thing: The honeymoon was over.

I had always thought that our relationship was unique. We had the kind of against-all-odds love you read about in romance novels. Only Nicholas was no hunky Fabio look-alike, and I wasn't a buxom damsel in distress (except perhaps when the electronic breast pump was set too high). He was a preemie, and I was a hormonally imbalanced, sleep-deprived new mother. From the beginning, our love faced obstacles.

Nicholas' birth was like a Las Vegas-style wedding. We rushed into it after barely eight months of pregnancy instead of the usual nine. We skipped the reception, so he could get to the Neonatal Intensive Care Unit (NICU) for help with his breathing. It was like marrying Englebert Humperdinck on show night. The groom left to take care of business, while I called my parents with the good news.

We spent the first week largely apart. I visited him in the NICU several times a day, but at night, I went home without him. It made me wonder why any woman in her right mind would marry a convict. Sure, you know where he is at all times, but all the good behavior in the world isn't going to put him in your arms at night.

When Nicholas finally came home, I promised to hold him forever. And I did. At least I felt like I did. At three weeks old, he developed colic; holding him was the only thing that made him feel better. I held him for hours and hours, day and night, as he cried it out. I now know that "forever" is about three months long and doesn't include many opportunities for showering. Now that's love.

We got through much of the "in sickness" part of our vows just in time. I soon felt like I was about to face the "til death do you part" vow - sleep deprivation was killing me. In fact, I wondered a lot about the "in good times" part. It seems like we had skipped over it.

I finally decided to take charge of our relationship. I referred to a self-help book called, *Solve Your Child's Sleep Problems* which ought to be re-titled, *Women Who Love Their Babies Too Much, But Desire Sleep Even More*. There were tears (for both of us) and a few harsh words (aimed at the book's authors), but it worked, and soon, our relationship was back on track.

Right away, Nicholas started to rest his head on my shoulder and let out a little sigh. He'd share his graham crackers with me, which would have been more enjoyable if he hadn't sucked on them first. Between that and his habit of leaving little surprises for me - mostly in my shoes - I knew I was loved.

So I was shocked when my true love sunk his teeth into my shoulder. All right, so I wouldn't let him to put his hands in the pickle jar at the deli. But violence? I never saw it coming.

I suppose I should have seen the signs that he was straying. He flirted with the other moms at Playorena class. He began to spend more time with the guys - his stuffed bunny rabbits, his Tinky Winky doll and the cat. He even preferred his red convertible, a Radio Flyer wagon, to me.

Then one day, at the shoe store, he reached his hand up to hold mine - for the first time. As we slowly strolled around the store, hand-in-hand, I realized that he still loved me and always had. He just needed to grow, not just physically, but personally.

As we face toddlerhood together, I know Nicholas isn't my baby anymore. And I, thank God, am no longer a hormonally imbalanced, sleep-deprived new mother. The honeymoon is over, but our best years together are about to begin ... just as soon he stops shaking his head "no" whenever vegetables near his mouth. The vows mention good and bad times, but they say nothing about dinnertime.

Just a Minute!

Open Windows

The following is a conversation between my friend and her neighbor.

Friend: (*sheepish*) "Did you hear me yelling at my kids last night?"

Neighbor: (*horrified*) "No, why? Did you hear me?"

Follow Me

Chris, age four, and I were walking home in the snow from his big brother's bus stop.

Chris: "Look! I'm making paw prints!"

Me: "Only on the days you're beastly."

A Son is a Son … Will Boys and Bugs Be Enough for Me?

I must look like I need a daughter. When people see my two sons load my mascara and lipstick like tiny logs into toy dump trucks, they ask if I'm going to "try for a girl." Yet when people see my friend's son and daughter - one of each - they congratulate her on her "perfect family." I don't know why others view her situation as perfect. Maybe it's because she'll never be grilled about her reproduction plans when she's at the video store renting *I Love Big Machines 2*. I haven't been that lucky.

What's wrong with having two sons and no daughters? I'll never have to share my clothes (please, God), braid toy horse manes or fish flowered hair ties out of the bathtub drain (please, God). I won't have to search for a pink disco dress with matching boa for Barbie. Even better, I won't have to find a disco dress and boa for my teen-age daughter, while explaining that the white taffeta gown with the big blue bow I wore at her age was for my *prom*, not Halloween.

Girls.

After three years of watching backhoes dig and ants crawl, I'm not sure what I'd do with a daughter. I don't know much about girls, even though I was one. As a kid, I was a tomboy. I still am. I'm perfectly happy not owning a plastic cake that plays a wedding march, like the one I saw at my friend's house. "Here comes the bride?" How about, *There Goes a Garbage Truck?* That's more my style. Good thing, too. We own the video.

But as much as I love raising sons, I worry that they'll someday lose touch with me. As the saying goes, a daughter is a daughter for life, but a son is a son until he's got someone else to tell him to put his dirty glass in the dishwasher. A daughter drives you to your colonoscopy and remembers your wedding anniversary. A son blows in *after* Mother's Day with a potted plant from 7-Eleven and his dirty laundry.

Boys.

I talk to my mother every day. My brother, on the other hand, sends her cryptic e-mail messages, and then disappears for a few days. I can tell already that my sons have inherited their uncle's communication skills. When Nicholas was two years old, he and a girl, who was a few months younger, spotted a toy boat. He said, "Boat," - for the first time. She said, "Look, Mommy! It's a boat. It's a blue boat." I waited for her to tell us whether it was a replica of the U.S.S.

Constitution, while Nicholas repeated, "Boat." No matter. When that girl calls Nicholas in ten years, she'll do all the talking anyway. And in twenty years, she'll realize he's not listening.

Men.

If my sons won't call me when they're grown, will they take care of me when I'm old? I haven't yet seen any signs of nurturing from them. At a playground sandbox one day, I watched a little girl fuss over a crying baby. Every time that infant wailed, the girl dropped her shovel and showed concern for him. My son, Chris, was concerned, too - over why the toy dump truck had only three wheels. The baby cried. The girl fussed. Chris searched for the missing wheel. At least my car will be taken care of.

Yet, perhaps I'm wrong about my sons - and sons in general. I found stark proof in my friend's husband that sons can take care of their mothers, when his mom discovered she was dying of cancer. He consulted doctors, scheduled surgeries and consoled his sister, who was seven-months pregnant. Then, at night, he slept on his mother's floor. In time, he handled the funeral arrangements. I don't need a daughter. I need a son like him.

I'm not going to try for a girl, because a daughter won't make my family complete. What I need are some rocks with good splash potential. My sons love to drop them in the street drain in front of the house. And I could use an insect identification book for our bug hunts. But I'm certainly not going to touch any of the bugs we find, like my sons do. Yuk!

Women.

Just a Minute!

Top Five Reasons it's Great to Raise Boys

1. You'll never have to kill a bug again. You've got live-in exterminators.
2. Why pay for Wrestle-mania tickets when you've got it in your own living room?
3. Enjoy nature anytime. Just open your son's hamper, and smell the dirt.
4. You never did learn how to French-braid, anyway.
5. Finally, a man who loves you for who you are - no matter how you look.

Put It Down!

One late afternoon, the boys and I were waiting for the store clerk to wrap a baby gift. And waiting. And waiting.

First, my sons entertained themselves by playing with all the baby toys on a nearby shelf. Then they rearranged the display of refrigerator magnets. Then they uncurled the decorative curly ribbons so conveniently located at child-level.

Store clerk: "So, what's it like having boys? I have two girls."

Oh, you'll find out when you reach for a decorative curly ribbon later, lady.

Outside Influences: Mommy as Human V-Chip

My three year old pretends his Lincoln Logs are peace pipes. It didn't occur to him to smoke his toys until after he saw *Peter Pan*, the classic film that features grown Native Americans sharing tobacco with children.

I gave Nicholas a smoking-is-bad-for-you speech, and then crossed my fingers when the assigned color for his preschool's Show and Tell was brown. Thankfully, he brought a brown stuffed bunny to school. No peace pipes at Circle Time. Not yet, anyway ... the outside influences are moving in. I hope I can beat them to my son.

When my five-year-old niece planned to dress up as Britney

(I'm-not-that-innocent) Spears for Halloween, I groaned. Lucky for me, Nicholas chose a teddy bear costume. He wouldn't know Britney Spears from Henry Kissinger. But I can't keep it that way for long, unless we move to Amish country.

Everywhere we go, negative outside influences are moving in. The TV at our local pizza shop shows CNN. I don't take Nicholas there when another skirmish breaks out in the Middle East or a scandal emerges from Washington. I don't want to have to explain air raids or the likes of Monica Lewinsky to my inquisitive pre-schooler. It's hard enough explaining how Cookie Monster can smell his Oreos even though he doesn't have a nose.

I skip the food court at the mall altogether, so Nicholas can't see Destiny's Child demonstrate what they mean by "Bootylicious" on the giant TV screen that shows music videos there. If we want to watch TV, we'd stay home, thank you. But we certainly wouldn't watch MTV. After twenty years, I still can't explain MTV to my parents, let alone to my child.

At the electronics store recently, I heard a so-called "clean" version of Slim Shady's "Just Don't Give a @#&!" coming from the stereo section. Now, I'm not asking to hear, "What the World Needs Now is Love," everywhere I go, but please, Slim (Warning: Explicit Lyrics) Shady? I went into the store looking for a cellular phone, and left needing a nice long drag on a Lincoln Log.

I don't know if it's gotten harder since I was a kid to block adverse outside influences, or if it just seems harder, because now I'm the parent. I can imagine how my parents must have felt two decades ago when my brother brought home a KISS record entitled, *Love Gun*. Love Gun? It's not exactly the kind of tune you serenade your date with at the malt shop. Poor Mom and Dad.

Poor me. Even the movies I watched as a kid don't seem appropriate for children anymore, at least not for my children. Some of today's G-rated films aren't much better. The bad guys - and sometimes the good ones - smoke, and a few films have more death and destruction than a Quentin Tarantino movie. The videos' boxes claim they're "fun for the entire family." Whose family? The Manson Family?

As a teenager, I wanted Tipper Gore to stay away from my entertainment. Now I want her to come over and install a V-Chip into my son's brain. In fact, if she could persuade him and his friends to dress up as teddy bears for Halloween until they're too old to trick or treat, I'd be grateful. I wouldn't know what to do if a group of pint-sized Britney Spears came to our door to pick Nicholas up, except perhaps, check the real estate listings in Amish country.

I know it's my job to keep the negative outside influences away from my son for as long as I can. And I'll certainly ban some films, avoid certain TV shows and screen the lyrics to music at home. Yet, I can't keep his friends from exposing him to what I don't want him to see or hear. And who knows what they're watching and listening to these days. Probably KISS, but I'd rather not know. Not yet, anyway.

For now, I'll relish my son's vanishing innocence, and hide some of his videotapes for a few years. But even pre-school's influences will start to affect him soon. When he stops drawing in his favorite color - pink - and starts scribbling in heavy black crayon like other boys in his class do, I'll know what happened.

I'm not sure who will miss pink more, Nicholas or me. I have a feeling though, it'll be me. And I doubt I'll be able to explain that to him, either - until one day, when those outside influences start moving in on his children.

Just a Minute!

Nothing On

My husband was getting the kids ready for bed, when Chris, age four, suddenly appeared behind me at my desk in the basement. He asked if he could call his grandmother to tell her about his first day of school. I turned around to say yes, only to find that he was completely nude.

I guess I shouldn't be concerned that he likes to phone naked for another ten years or so.

Amen

Chris was saying his prayers the other night before bed. His first prayer was for his pal, Ryan. I was so touched, I kissed him, and commended him for thinking of his friend. So I thought maybe he'd pray for his father or for me if I asked. "Is there anyone else special you'd like to pray for tonight?" I asked.

"Yeah," he replied. "God bless Scooby-Doo."

The Cool Mom:
How My Son and I Learned to Like Each Other Again

If the other neighborhood moms only knew. I'm not really Cool Mom like they think I am. Sure, I'm the only mom who actually drops to the ground when "we all fall down" during, "Ring Around the Rosie." And I'm the mom who taught some of the kindergarteners how to play the *Spiderman* theme song on kazoos. I even took a spectacular cannonball dive at a pre-school graduation pool party. After I emerged from the water to applause, one mom asked me, "Are you this much fun at home?" I was too ashamed to tell her the truth. At home, I wasn't a cool mom. I was a screaming maniac.

Everything I knew about discipline wasn't working with Nicholas, then five. I tried time outs. I tried rewards and consequences. I tried shouting until the light fixtures rattled. And still, my son kept whining.

Mostly, he whined about the food I put on his plate. Apparently, "yucky" foods, such as fruits and vegetables, would be more appealing if they were shaped like cartoon characters. And since I never found a carrot shaped like Batman, every meal was a battle between my son and me.

On some days, Nicholas whined about pretty much everything that didn't go his way. He whined when I wouldn't let him wear his "Carnivore!" T-shirt to church. He threw a fit when I couldn't fix the toy his little brother had broken while I was busy trying to make string cheese look like little *Star Wars* light sabers. Then he whined about the light sabers.

One day, I couldn't stand fighting anymore, so I ran away. Sort of. I begged my husband to come home early from work one afternoon so I could escape, alone.

At the bookstore, I searched the parenting section for advice. When I saw another woman leafing through *Fun with Mommy and Me,* I hid my copy of *How to Behave So Your Children Will, Too!*

While she was, perhaps, looking up how to make sock puppets, I was trying to figure out how to make it through an hour or two without the veins popping out of my neck like the Incredible Hulk's.

I needed help.

My mother-in-law advised me to be firm with Nicholas, as though shouting, "No! Absolutely Not! No Way, Jose! No! No! No!" was just me being a pushover. My mother suggested I ignore him when he whines, much like, I suppose, one would ignore a Mack truck following you around the highway, honking its horn and flashing its lights.

Instead, I called a local expert who runs Positive Parenting classes in my town. He observed us in our house for a few hours, and then gave me some tips for behaving so my children would, too.

He taught me how to teach Nicholas to accept "no" for an answer, first through role-play, then with real-life situations. If my son didn't accept no, I sent him to his room the moment his whining started, and remained unemotional when doling out the discipline.

But I also praised Nicholas every time he accepted that he couldn't wear his favorite Spiderman sweatshirt on a ninety-degree day or eat just crescent rolls and Girl Scout cookies for dinner. Most importantly, I stuck with the plan, every day, all day long, even when my little Mack truck wasn't cooperating.

After a few days, I stopped screaming. After a few weeks, Nicholas stopped whining all the time. After a while, we started liking each other as much as we loved each other.

But I didn't tell anyone about it. I was too embarrassed.

Then one day, a neighbor sheepishly admitted she felt like she was yelling at her son all the time. She thought she was the only one making the light fixtures rattle. I set her straight. Then I told her what had worked for me.

All moms lose their cool with their kids now and then. But when you can't get it back, you need to get help. The moms who do are truly cool moms.

At soccer practice last weekend, I was the only coach who taught her team to shout, "Gooooooooaaaallll!" when they scored. While all the other teams were quietly practicing dribbling and passing, my players were throwing their arms in the air, running around in circles and shouting like the Brazilian national soccer team at the World Cup.

Nicholas raced past me, shouting, "Cool, Mom!" Yeah. I know.

Just a Minute!

The Four Food Groups According to My Five-Year-Old

1. Breads and cakes
2. Apple juice
3. Girl Scout cookies
4. Anything shaped like a cartoon character

Welcome Home, Mom

My in-laws watched the kids for a few days while I went on vacation with my mother. (Thanks Omi and Opa.)

When they dropped the kids off, my boys immediately began bickering over toys and stood on their heads on the couch.

I sighed. My mother-in-law snickered, "Welcome to your world." Then she left.

Someone's in the Kitchen with Mommy: The Way to a Boy's Heart

My son wants to be a "cookerman" when he grows up. Not a baseball player or a doctor or Bob the Builder like every other five-year-old. No, my Christopher wants to be Emeril Lagasse - and he wants me to teach him how. So I'm forsaking my quick and easy recipes that get me out the kitchen as fast as possible to cultivate my budding chef's love for cooking. In the process, I'm learning that cooking isn't the chore I've always thought it to be. Not when you're cooking with Christopher, anyway.

When Nicholas was Chris's age, he collected dinosaur books like the rest of the boys in his pre-school class. Not Chris. He saves supermarket circulars and cuts Hamburger Helper ads out of my magazines. Every morning, he asks, "What's for dinner?" And he's the only kid I know who actually enjoys grocery shopping. Most five year olds have learned all the letters of the alphabet. My son also knows the names of all the spices in my pantry.

But until I started mixing and basting with Chris, I viewed cooking much as I do vacuuming: it's a dirty job, but somebody's gotta do it. The plaque that once hung on my mother's kitchen wall sums up how I've always felt about making dinner: "Why cook for TWO HOURS when everybody eats for just TWO MINUTES?"

Yet now I've got a child who suddenly appears in the kitchen when he hears me taking out pots and pans to ask, "Can I cook with you?" I can't say no. Whether we're preparing filet mignon or reheating yesterday's meatloaf, it's all a culinary treat to Christopher. Thanks to him, I'm learning to see it that way, too.

To Chris, grating cheese is as much fun as riding a bike and cracking eggs is as enjoyable as playing in the kiddie pool. Serving homemade pizza with all the toppings is as satisfying as crossing the monkey bars for the first time. The boy sure loves cooking.

I guess I shouldn't be surprised that my son is so food-obsessed. His father watches the Food Network like other men watch ESPN. He plans weekend meals by searching the Internet for the best recipes. He cooks nearly the entire Thanksgiving dinner himself. And, for our summer barbecues, he spends an entire day preparing ribs that make every guest beg for his recipe.

In short, he gets the glory meals. I get the tuna casserole on a Tuesday night because it's the only meal I can fit in between soccer practice and the PTA meeting. Nobody's ever oohed and aahed over my fish sticks and peas.

But thanks to my little cookerman, I'm discovering my own inner Emeril. Together, Chris and I have made Dill and Honey Mustard Meatloaf, Mediterranean Chicken, Chocolate Chip Blondies, a birthday cake shaped like a volcano, and Sea Bass with Hoisin Sauce. I never even knew what hoisin sauce was until I started cooking with Christopher. Now I know my way around the International Foods Section of the supermarket the way I used to know what time the deli manager put out the ready-made chickens.

The same woman who once thought that chili was an exotic meal because it contains more than three ingredients now cooks Kushiyaki, Japanese-style shish kabobs. I buy cookbooks with recipes that take longer than twenty minutes to prepare. I volunteer to bake lemon poppy seed bread for the school bake sale because I think it'd be fun to make. And I treat Chris to dinner at hibachi-style restaurants so he can see the "cookermen" in action.

Just the other day, Chris and I were walking through a parking lot when he stopped, smiled and shouted, "I smell cooking!" I smelled it, too. We tried to guess what food it was. I thought it was nutmeg, but Chris blurted, "Butterscotch!" He was right. I promised to look for a recipe with butterscotch in it that we could make together. Then we walked through the parking lot silently, both enjoying the smell of cooking.

Now when Chris asks, "What's for dinner?" I answer, "How about one of your Mexican recipes?" Then we make quesadillas together and maybe even some brownies for dessert. I can't wait to watch him pour the black beans into a bowl, or dollop sour cream onto the tortillas. It makes him so happy. And it makes me absolutely thrilled that someday, he just might take over all the cooking in our house.

Just a Minute!

Fruits and Veggies

Not only does Chris want to be a chef for Halloween, he wants to be one when he grows up. That's why, while all the other kids in church were scribbling in their Batman or Dora, the Explorer coloring books last Sunday, Chris was thumbing through a *Harry and David* catalog. The kid behind us colored in the Batmobile. Chris eyed the Fruit of the Month Club selections.

Food, Glorious Food!

Christopher loves cooking. He also loves to collect pictures of food, so I let him have the supermarket circulars that come in the mail. When we don't have any of those, I let him have my old women's magazines, so he can cut out the pictures of "Apple-Asparagus Casserole" and staple them to photos of "Double Chocolate Tarts."

All the other boys in the neighborhood are cutting out pictures of Major League Baseball players or backhoes. My son collects pictures of crudités.

Twelve Ways to Measure How You're Doing, Mom

Not sure whether you're doing a good job as mom? Here are twelve ways that prove you're doing a good job.

1. You've had about seventeen consecutive minutes of sleep since the baby was born last month, and yet you can remember your name and the name of that guy next to you who's snoring through the baby's cries.

2. One word: Episiotomy.

3. You calm your sick toddler by singing "You Are My Sunshine" - after he's thrown up Spaghettios all over you.

4. Your children are wearing socks that - at least from afar - appear to match.

5. The bottom of your purse is filled with Chuck E. Cheese's tokens, those teeny little barrettes shaped like bows and Goldfish cracker crumbs.

6. You look forward to your kid's pediatrician appointments, because to you, they count as outings.

7. Two words: Potty training.

8. You're so tired, you tell your three-year-old to flush his hands and wash the toilet, and he knows enough not to do it.

9. All day, you bake cookies, play Candy Land, and make forts out of couch cushions with the kids, who thank you by cheering, "Daddy's home!" And yet, you don't go retrieve the newspaper's help wanted section from the birdcage.

10. You spend the afternoon helping your daughter match up her Barbie's twenty-three pairs of little, plastic shoes, when you don't even have time to match a pair of your own.

11. You camp out overnight for preschool registration, much like you used to do for Springsteen tickets.

12. When your kindergartener wipes off your good-bye kiss with the back of his hand, you don't grab him and scream, "Who are you, and what have you done with my baby?!"

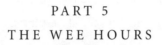

PART 5
THE WEE HOURS

Fifteen Signs that Mommy Needs a Little More "Me" Time

1. You've decided not to wash the red paint from today's art project off your fingers, because it's the closest thing to a manicure you've had all year.

2. You talk to the radio, because deejays are pretty much the only adults who talk to you all day (besides Joe from *Blues Clues*).

3. Your purse is a diaper bag with little yellow duckies on it - even though your youngest has been potty-trained for months.

4. Your snooze alarm is a wallop in the head every ten minutes by a small leg in Barney feety pajamas.

5. You reach into your pocket to pay the Starbucks cashier, but all you find are a handful of Chuck E. Cheese's tokens and a Hot Wheel tire.

6. You know all the words to the *Dora, the Explorer* theme song, but can't for the life of you remember what the title of your wedding song was, let alone the lyrics.

7. When it's your turn to hide in Hide 'N Seek, you bring a flashlight and reading material.

8. When it's the kids' turn to hide, you don't seek. At least not until your coffee is done.

9. You don't recognize any of the movie names on the cinema marquee, except the animated features, which you've seen three times each.

10. You finally decide to go to dinner without the kids, only to find out your babysitter moved cross-country last fall.

11. You're jealous of the cat because she gets more sleep in one day than you usually get in a week.

12. The only way you can tell the difference between nine in the morning and nine at night is to look out the window for daylight or darkness.

13. You rigged the baby monitor backwards so you can at least hear *American Idol* while you're trying to get the baby to fall back asleep (again).

14. Your idea of regular exercise is a nightly chase after your screaming, naked toddler at bath time.

15. You've designed your own advent calendar that counts down to the first day of school in September.

The Little Things: One Mom's Look at the Other Side of the Fence

I'm beginning to think I squandered my twenties. Maybe I should have spent the decade before motherhood doing exciting things like hiking the Himalayas, dancing in mosh pits and trying out for game shows. Now that I'm a (thirty-something) mother of two, it's tough to take snowboarding lessons or camp out for Springsteen tickets. These days, I camp out only for preschool registration.

But my child-free friends from college have no problem flying to faraway places and doing exciting things. And yet, that's not why I envy them.

During a college reunion weekend, I watched videos of one old pal skydiving and heli-skiing. First, she leaped out of an airplane over Australia. Then she jumped from a helicopter over the Rockies. The only jumping I've done lately is over the poop at the petting zoo.

While I haven't flown on an airplane since before my kids were born, my friends seem to have traveled the world. I listened quietly as they told stories about their trips to such exotic places as China and Vietnam.

One friend remarked that it was funny how she'd eat whatever the natives eat, even though she'd never touch it at home. "I know," I said, "I feel the same way at Chuck E. Cheese's." She had never even heard of Chuck E. Cheese's. She doesn't know what she's missing.

But the trans-continental trips and extreme sports didn't make me jealous of my friends. I envied them, because they get to sit down for long periods of time. And they don't even have to retrieve the couch cushions from the toy box first. They can talk on the phone without someone hanging from their belt loops, sobbing something alarming about gummy worms and the VCR. And to top it off, my friends are so seemingly clueless about just how wonderful such small freedoms are.

I watched my friends walk into a store, buy what they needed and go home. For me, it's rarely that easy. While at a stationery store, I innocently cleaned up the party hats my two year old had strewn across an aisle. Bad idea. While he had a very dramatic, very public, temper tantrum, I hid in the nearby greeting card section, where I found a wonderful Bon Voyage card. If only my toddler could read.

When my friends went out, they put on their coats, grabbed their keys and left. When I take my kids out, it's more like WrestleMania meets Major League Baseball's contract negotiations. Getting my two year old into his coat, shoes and car seat is like trying to stuff a greased pig into a Spiderman costume. Getting my four year old to put down his toys and climb into the car is like persuading Sammy Sosa to come down a million dollars a year. By the time we finally get out of the driveway, I'm sweating as though I've taken an aerobics class. If only I had the time.

I knew what I was in for when I traded the chance to go skydiving, take safaris and drive sports cars for motherhood. It really doesn't bother me that my childfree sister-in-law saw Hootie and the Blowfish in concert, while I saw them only on *Sesame Street.* I don't care to take up scuba diving or eat strange food in Asia. I just want to be able to take a shower without having to open the door and put the wheels back on a toy dump truck.

Like my friends, I didn't appreciate how much time I had for myself - until it was gone. Recently on one long, rainy afternoon, I hid in the kitchen, alphabetizing the spices, while the kids watched Peter Pan. No one looked for me for forty-five minutes. That's a mini-vacation to me, and I didn't have to leap from an aircraft to get it. It's the little things that make this mom happy. Lucky for me, as the big things are still out of reach.

Soon after my reunion weekend, my family came down with the flu. I spent the nights comforting the sick and the days hovering over mugs of Theraflu. Very early one morning, my toddler had finally fallen back asleep in my arms, when I sneezed and awakened him. I prepared for a long session of calming him back down, when he simply kissed me and said, "Bwess you."

Like I said, it's the little things. My friends don't know what they're missing.

Just a Minute!

Achoo!

One day, I sneezed while driving my mini-van, but no one in the back seat said a word.

So I asked, "What do you say when someone sneezes?"

Chris, age three, answered, "It's too loud!"

Island Night

My friend, Liane, has no children, so she and her husband can travel often. She recently returned from a cruise to Costa Rica, where, she said, she saw parrots, toucans and sloths up in the palm trees.

I, on the other hand, went to our community's "Island Night," where I saw (paper) parrots and toucans in (inflatable) palm trees. The sloths sat at the bar all night.

The Good Old Days:
Why I'll Take Lollipops Over Lullabies Any Day

I have a confession to make: I don't like babies all that much. I know, mothers aren't supposed to say such things. But, to me, babies are like puppies: they're lovable and cute - as long as they go home with someone else to drool on their sofa and wake them up at five in the morning.

While I've always loved my babies, I *like* them better now that they're old enough to kick a ball, sob with me when the spider dies on *Charlotte's Web* and help me make chocolate chip cookies. I like them more now, because they have passion. My babies didn't have passion. My babies had gas.

It wasn't easy admitting that I don't care for babies. After all, aren't all mothers supposed to love holding babies? Well, I held my colicky babies for hours and hours for months and months.

In fact, one day, I patted Christopher's back for four hours, until he finally fell asleep in my arms. When I tried to get Nicholas, then only twenty months old, to get me a blanket for my cold feet, he brought me a half-eaten Pop Tart, a toy pick-up truck, the *TV Guide* - everything but the blanket.

I sat there, hopelessly trapped, watching my toddler take inventory of the living room, when I should have been taking him to the playground. I wondered where the Little League games were, the carnival rides, the Christmas pageants. Where was the mini-van packed with the winning peewee soccer team? Where was the motherhood I thought I would have? Certainly not in the recliner, trying not to wake my fussy baby, fantasizing about a nice, warm pair of tube socks.

When other moms coo over a baby and ask "Don't you miss it?" I don't dare answer. I don't want them to know that, unlike them, I don't linger in the layette section at Babies "R" Us. I do, however, cry at baby shampoo commercials, because it reminds me how far I've come from when attaining proper footwear was my highest goal of the day. But I can't tell them that.

When my kids were babies, I never wondered why fish don't have eyebrows, what the inside of a tennis ball looks like or why backhoes are usually yellow. I just wondered when I could get a nap.

But now that my sons are older, there's much more to wonder about, much more to be passionate about, than REM sleep and infant gas relief drops.

When my husband and I took our kids at four and two-and-a-half on their first trip to nearby New York City to see *Blues Clues Live*, the boys loved the city more than the show. We could have saved the $200 for tickets, and wandered around mid-town checking out the taxis, fountains, hot dog vendors and crowds.

My kids made me see Manhattan the way I hadn't seen it since visiting my dad's office there twenty-five years earlier. They brought back the sense of wonder I had lost while wondering where my socks were.

Now, there are driveways to color with chalk. There are garbage trucks to wave to, and there are scented candles to smell at the card store. There are worms to collect. (Okay, I don't share *all* their passions.) And there's a rainbow up in the sky. "Did you see it, Mommy?" Yes - now that I have the energy to lift my head above the horizon - yes, I did.

Sure, I have to wash chocolate ice cream stains out of their shirts. And I sometimes have to explain to a wailing kid why he can't have the red sprinkle-covered cookie shaped like Elmo's head for lunch. But, overall, we've come a long way. Besides, I get to hear them refer to sprinkles as "sprinklers."

Perhaps a better mom would be more wistful about her kids' bygone baby years. I know what they say about children: the days are long, but the years are short. Well, I must confess: I'm finally glad the days are long, because the good old days have just begun, and I want them to last.

Just a Minute!

Return Trip

Chris, age five: "When we're grown-ups, we can come back to Sea World."

Nicholas, age seven: "Yeah, but when we're grown-ups, I don't think we'll want to."

Let it Snow

It was snowing and windy one afternoon when I picked Christopher up from pre-school. A sudden gush of wind blew snow in my face, so I quickly turned my back to avoid it.

Not Christopher. He was running into the wind, hat off, eyes closed and tongue sticking out, trying to catch the snow in his mouth.

Ah, to be five again. And to be able to run with my eyes closed.

While They're Little:
Learning to Enjoy the Flying Animal Cracker Years

It happens everyday, everywhere I go. At the supermarket, the deli, the post office, people keep telling me to enjoy my kids while they're little. "You mean it doesn't get any better than this?" I ask, while my four year old lobs animal crackers over his little brother who buries his sippy cup in a store display. But these people, usually veteran moms, just smile and leave, home to their Pop-Tart-free sofas and restful nights. Maybe if they found donkey-shaped cookies or melted M&Ms in their hair every night they'd remember what it was *really* like when their kids were little. I'll never forget.

Perhaps they've forgotten the less-than-pleasant parts of their children's early years - the parts that have been making my days seem so long. Either that, or they're hazing their kids' generation - the generation that kept them from eating a full meal or getting a night's sleep thirty years ago. Let me assure you, ladies, my kids are settling the score for you.

If only they'd think back to when they spent their days wiping toothpaste murals off the walls and fielding relentless questions about everything from why we have two eyes, but only one nose, to whether there are potties in heaven. I go to the supermarket to get the heck out of the house. Unless you know why cats have tails, leave me alone.

Don't these seasoned moms remember being trapped in the house with a toddler who put the phone in the refrigerator and a four year old who wouldn't eat without a promise to remove the raisins from his cinnamon-raisin bagel or the bananas from his banana bread? I do. It happened last Monday - and Tuesday and Wednesday, too. I guess if it had occurred only as recently as 1972, it would be harder to recall, much like the reasons I became a mother were last Monday, Tuesday and Wednesday.

Yet I caught a glimpse of what people have been trying to tell me when I took my kids to the children's museum. It was the first time we went there without a diaper bag, baby bottles or a stroller.

Time had flown by after all. It had just felt slow, like pulling a tooth or writing a check to the IRS.

While I watched my sons paint a picture in the art exhibit, I felt sad. I thought about how they'll both be in pre-school this fall, where they'll paint without me. They'll explore without me, learn without me, sing without me and laugh without me. Okay, so they'll also whine without me, but they'll be without me, and I'll miss them. My babies, I realized, weren't babies anymore. For the first time, that made me a little teary-eyed.

Suddenly, my thoughts were interrupted by two seven year olds in firefighter boots from one museum exhibit and plastic knights' helmets from another, carrying a giant rubber snake. They barreled past my two little boys like Mac trucks through a small town on a Sunday morning. I swore I'd stop snorting sarcastically when people tell me to enjoy my kids while they're little. I've seen the future, and it's wielding a rubber python in the ballet exhibit. Today is looking better already.

I'm paying more attention to the moments that won't happen when my kids are older. I'm relishing when Chris looked up to the sky one morning and exclaimed, "Wow! The moon!" In a few years, it'll take a rare Pokémon card or an MTV van - or whatever the kids are into - to get him that excited. I'm cherishing when Nicholas put down his fork at dinner and asked, "Mommy, how are you doing?" A decade from now, he might not care.

When they're in grade school, they won't want to hold my hand anymore. As junior high schoolers, they won't hug me and say, "I love you, too." In high school, they won't even want to be seen with me. And then they'll both be gone. And I'll wander through the supermarket, the deli and the post office alone, warning young mothers to enjoy their kids while they're little. I hope they'll listen.

Just a Minute!

Night Wakings

One night, I found a Pokémon stuck to Chris's sweaty head while he slept. I removed it and put it on his nightstand.

At 3 A.M., he shouted, "Where's my Pokémon card?!" I leaped out of bed, handed him his card and waited for my heart to stop racing before returning to bed.

Next time, I'm taping the darn thing to his hand.

I Love You?

I was in the basement when I heard Chris yelling to me from upstairs.

Me: "What?!"
Chris: (faint sound)
Me: "What? I love you? Awww, thanks. I love you, too, honey!"
Nicholas (at the top of the stairs): (*like he's talking to the Village Idiot*) "No, Mom. He said he's *hungry*."

Oh.

Mommy's Sabbatical:
My Much Needed Vacation from Being Needed

No wonder I find my morning teacup in the microwave oven most nights. It turns out that the average pre-schooler demands Mom's attention *every four minutes*. With two little kids at home with me during the day, the time I have for myself doesn't last much longer than a television commercial break.

After five years of short breaks, I decided I needed a longer one. So I took a week-long sabbatical from my job as a stay-at-home mom. It was the best thing I've ever done for myself - and for my kids.

I had become so tired of being needed every four minutes that I actually fell asleep during *Dragon Tales Live*, a loud musical production held in an arena full of twenty thousand shrieking pre-schoolers. My head started bobbing soon after the bubbly announcer asked, "Do you know why we're so happy?" And I answered, "Too much Prozac?" I was so punchy that I was heckling a show for three year olds.

In any other job, if you suddenly zonked out at your desk or on the assembly line or at a store's cash register, you'd get a day or two off.

But at-home moms don't get vacation days. Just a few hours here and there, maybe a weekend if a grandmother takes the kids overnight. But rarely an entire, honest-to-goodness week off like "people who work" get twice a year or more.

So when my husband and kids packed the car for a beach vacation with my in-laws, I opted to stay home. Alone. Drinking a cup of hot tea slooooooowly. Until I finished the very…last …drop. Then I spent the rest of the week doing what I usually can't: remaining seated through entire meals, sleeping through the night and making phone calls without once shouting "I'm on the phone!" or "Get off your brother!"

I even got rid of the cat for a day, sending him to the vet to get his teeth cleaned. One friend remarked, "Geez, Jen. What if you had a fish?" I replied, "He'd be visiting his cousins in the lake this week."

I didn't want anyone to need me. Not every four minutes. Not the way little children need you - while you're freeing the toilet of what appears to be your scrap-booking supplies; or while you're wrestling the cat into his carrier; or when you, God forbid, close the bathroom door between you and them.

I wanted to be responsible for just me for just one week.

When I told my friends about my sabbatical from motherhood they all asked the same question: "Are you going to join your family at the shore mid-week?" Huh? So I asked, "If your boss finally gave you a week off after *half-a-decade* without a vacation, would you return to the office on Wednesday?"

No one answered me. Then I realized what everyone must have thought: I was having a nervous breakdown.

Moms aren't supposed to want to be away from their kids. That's why there's a quirky sign in the Toys "R" Us parking lot reserving spots for "Dads Who Would Rather Be Somewhere Else," but nonesuch for moms.

And at-home moms aren't supposed to complain about their jobs, not with so many moms working for paychecks just to make ends meet these days. The job of an at-home mom, practically mandatory in my mother's day, has become a privilege to many. And no one wants to hear the privileged complain - even if their "privilege" is to endure a toddler meltdown over a package of marshmallow chicks at the supermarket. Twice.

At-home moms need to recharge their batteries just like everybody else. My sabbatical let me store up enough energy to return to my 24/7 job. It helped me refill my well the way I never seem to be able to refill my teacup.

I love my kids so much I took one week off from taking care of them so I could be a better mother the other fifty-one weeks of the year. And after seven days of taking care of just me, I was ready to return to work.

My kids missed me that week (and I missed them), but they appreciated me more when they returned. Because once again, I was gung-ho to spend my days reading *The Colossal Book of Dinosaurs*. Three times in a row. To make Play-Doh worms and paper maché volcanoes (and to clean it all up). Twice. And to drop everything to search for a beloved security blanket. Every four minutes.

Just a Minute!

Just a Dream

Sea World Orlando, 5:11 P.M.

I saw a pregnant woman pushing a screaming toddler in a stroller while her husband dragged a four-foot stuffed Scooby-Doo doll in a Santa outfit behind them.

I had a nightmare like that once.

Glasses for the Eyes in the Back of My Head

While overseeing a playdate for three little boys, I noticed a pile of crumbs in the living room. I took out the vacuum and cleaned up the crumbs for just FOUR MINUTES.

I turned off the vacuum to discover that two of the boys had lugged my office chair almost all the way up the basement stairs, calling it "Jimmy Neutron's ship," while the third boy was hanging from the stair rails, singing.

"What?" I said. "No time to start a fire? Or flood the basement, perhaps?"

A Half Hour by the Sea:
Detachment Parenting for the Modern Mom

I'm starting a new trend called "detachment parenting." No, not attachment parenting, where a parent - usually a mother - walks around all day with her child strapped to her body, creating a special bonding experience between her and her chiropractor. I mean detachment parenting, where a mom like me, who spends upwards of fourteen hours a day with her kids, gets a little time to herself every day - and doesn't feel guilty about it.

When I was a teenager I worked a summer job at a clothing warehouse that had a sign that read, "Take Frequent Breaks." I spent my days counting sweaters, seated, and yet my bosses wanted me to take time off every now and then to stretch and chitchat about who shot J.R. on "Dallas."

But stay-at-home moms have no Take Frequent Breaks rule. At least, I didn't. When my kids were very little, I planned every moment of every day so my sons could get all the benefits of having a stay-at-home mother.

We put puzzles together. We played with toy cars. We drew roads in chalk on the driveway. We built forts where we'd watch the video *I Love Big Machines* together. We'd color, paint, make cookies and mold replicas of the "Blues Clues" cast in Play-Doh.

At times, we looked like a magazine picture: mother and children spending quality time together making caterpillars out of egg cartons. Other times, though, we looked like a scene from *Lord of the Flies*: cranky children holding exhausted mother hostage simply because she dared to leave the room to check her e-mail. Too much of the former caused the latter.

One day, when my older son clung to me, refusing to take a swim lesson, I explained to another mother that he didn't get much time without me. She thought that was wonderful. If she didn't have to work, she said, she'd never leave her children. I tried to feel lucky, but all I felt were Nicholas' nails digging into my thigh.

I must admit, a part of me loved my children's theatrics when I left them with a relative so I could get a haircut. It made me feel important. It justified my role as stay-at-home mom. I was their life support system. Pull the plug, and the whole family suffers.

Meanwhile, I suffocated.

I actually felt guilty for doing housework. Laundry was taking time away from making every moment of my children's formative years an enriching, educational experience, as parenting experts advocate. How could I fold underwear, when my children needed me to point out the colors and shapes in *Good Night Moon*?

Yet what my kids really needed now and then was to shove rocks into their toy trucks. Or to wrestle each over the Rockin' Elmo doll. Or to put all the magnets on and off the refrigerator door over and over. They might not learn their A, B, Cs by age two, but they'd learn how to fend for themselves. And that's more important, because I won't always be there for them.

Last summer, we took a week-long family trip to Martha's Vineyard where my children slowly turned into beasts by Wednesday. I left the kids with my husband, hopped on my bike and rode seven miles to Chappaquiddick, a relatively remote island off Martha's Vineyard, accessible by a short ferry ride.

After I pedaled to the other side of the island to a virtually deserted beach, I took off my shoes, socks and shirt, and waded in wearing my sports bra and shorts. I heard only the waves, the seagulls and an occasional passing of a tourist's plane.

I felt like Joan Anderson in *A Year By the Sea*, the memoir of a woman who took a year off from her family. But I could only get a half-hour. Still, that was enough.

I realized my kids aren't going to remember the egg carton caterpillars. They're going to remember that I was tired all the time. Tired and unhappy. If I didn't enrich my own life, how could I enrich theirs?

As I floated in Nantucket Sound, I promised myself to "Take Frequent Breaks" every day. To start detachment parenting to make my kids less attached to me. And to not feel guilty about it.

My kids have adjusted well. In time, they realized that Mommy isn't available every moment of every day. That she needs breaks. That it's fun to take the magnets off the refrigerator while Mommy checks her e-mail. And that she's never making egg carton caterpillars again.

Eyes

Chris was getting bored in church one Sunday, so he counted my facial features.

Chris, age five: "You have two eyes."
Me: "Don't forget the eyes in the back of my head."

Hot Wheels

On the road one weekend afternoon, my husband and I spotted a car with a strange title on the back: Entervan.

Me: "But I think it's a Dodge Caravan."
Pete: "I think that's the name of the custom stereo system."
Me: "Oh God. I can tell one mini-van from another."

What I Did All Day:
Only Thirteen Hours, Forty-five Minutes Until Bedtime!

People never ask my husband, "Do you work?" Yet, they ask me. If I answer, "No," it implies I sit around watching "A Wedding Story" on cable TV, or read fashion magazines and work on my tan. If I say, "Yes," it sounds presumptuous. After all, I'm home during the day, so I must have a lot of free time, right?

Yet for all anyone knows, my husband played Minesweeper on his computer and made hot toddies in the company kitchen all day. I, on the other hand, entertained two little boys who think the VCR makes a nice piggy bank.

Do I work? It sure feels like it.

Today, for example, was yet another sick day, so we all stayed home. Again. If I didn't keep a close eye on my sons, they'd turn into human tornadoes, tearing through the house and sending furniture into the treetops. They couldn't stay interested in any one activity for more than fifteen minutes. So, during the fourteen hours they were awake, I had to come up with eighty-six things to do - and clean it all up.

First, I offered to cut out of construction paper whatever shapes my kids wanted to paste down- quickly! Nicholas asked for a car, a volcano and a Tyrannosaurus Rex. He got something that looked like an ad for Rent-a-Wreck, a brown mountain with orange hair and a big green blob with teeth.

Chris wanted a pick-up truck, Santa Claus - in a black suit - and Shaggy from Scooby-Doo. He got a rectangle with wheels, a bearded man in what appeared to be black Capri pants and a big green blob with teeth.

Only thirteen hours, forty-five minutes until bedtime!

Then Nicholas decided we should make a castle out of a cardboard box. After we cut out windows and a drawbridge, and painted the box gray, I tried to draw tiny little lions and tiny little dragons on tiny little flags. Instead, I drew a kitten with walrus fangs and a fire-breathing salamander. Then I super-glued my finger to my cheek. My kids didn't notice, though, because it was time for the next activity.

The boys made four multi-colored birthday cakes out of Play-Doh, and sang, "Happy Birthday," to me four times. At that rate, I'd be old enough for a nursing home by lunchtime. Though frankly, a quiet game of mah-jongg sounded appealing.

While I cleaned that up, the kids relocated my Tupperware® to the space under the basement stairs. They told me the space was really a car repair shop and my Tupperware Snackatizer tray was really an eighteen-wheeler with a broken radiator.

I told myself our house was really Acapulco, and my kids were actually cabana boys taking a chaise-lounge to the beach for me.

They were running out of Tupperware; soon, they'd find my good china. In a panic, I suggested we make cookies - from scratch. While I rolled out a batch, the boys decorated another with colored sugar . . . tall piles of sugar that looked like giant volcanoes erupting from the dough.

I turned the sugar volcanoes into more manageable (and edible) hills, while they worked on the dough - with every kitchen tool they could find. I had dough on my turkey baster, meat thermometer, three spatulas, two serving spoons, a lemon zester and the "Have You Ever Been Mellow?" track on my Olivia Newton John CD.

Only thirteen hours, fifteen minutes until bedtime!

I sent the kids to the couch with some snacks and drinks. Then I scraped the glue, paint and sugar off my clothes, and joined them. We counted the birthday cakes they had made. We talked about the shapes on the castle - triangular flags, rectangular drawbridge, round kitten's - I mean, lion's - head. We named the colors of our sugar volcanoes. And we talked about what turkey basters are really for.

What I did all day is hard to measure, even in fifteen-minute increments. I suppose I kept the kids from tearing down the house. And I helped make a big mess.

But what I really did all day was give my children my time. Quantity time. Time for super-gluing little flags onto toothpicks. Time for making big, green blobs with teeth. It doesn't matter much to my kids, as long as I'm with them.

We sat on the couch, eating cookies and planning the rest of the day. With another thirteen hours ahead of us, there was a lot left to do.

Then we wondered what Daddy does all day at work.

Peter Rabbit

At the mall, I read a sign near the Easter Bunny photo center: "Bunny breaks from 3 - 4 P.M."

I'd like to post a sign, "Mommy breaks from 4 - 5 P.M. - and on Mother's Day."

What a Gas!

During one recent playdate, Nicholas and Auston, both age five, were burping at each other with those pathetic little kid burps that sound like the floor is squeaking.

I told them to stop. They burped. I told them again. They burped.

So, I said, "You think that's a burp? THIS is a burp." And then I let out the kind of burp my big brother taught me when I was ten. The kind of burp that Nickelodeon uses as a sound effect on Jimmy Neutron. The kind of burp no mother on my block has ever let go. Both boys fell to the ground laughing.

And THEN they stopped burping. They couldn't handle the competition.

Mommy's Fabulous Blue Dress:
Or How I Got My Groove Back at the Waldorf Astoria

"Well, it's a good thing I got you the Large," Pete said after he bought me a rather tight Mickey Mouse T-shirt during a business trip to Orlando. I'd have decked him, but I was too exhausted from taking care of our colicky newborn for a week - alone. As I struggled to pull poor Mickey's face over my swelling postpartum chest and stomach, I looked like a Mouseketeer after too many Dumbo ice cream pops and not enough sleep.

For years, I got used to looking and feeling, well, large, and worse, haggardly, until the night I wore a fabulous blue dress to a function at the Waldorf Astoria Hotel in New York City. That night, Mommy got her groove back. And she's been fighting to keep it ever since.

When our neighbors invited us to a fund-raiser at the Waldorf, we said yes. Was it about the fine dining, the ice sculptures, the enormous shrimp cocktail display, the socializing? Nah. For me, after six years of motherhood, it was all about the dress.

I had never attended a formal fund-raising affair before. My husband's small software company doesn't buy tickets for such events. And in my job as stay-at-home mom, formal means clothes without paint, dirt, peanut butter or marker on them.

I figured I would need some help picking out the dress, so I brought my mother along. As soon as we walked into Nordstrom's formalwear department, we both saw it: a baby blue, floor length, satin gown, with a train and lace straps.

We appeased the saleswoman and grabbed a few more practical black dresses, but Mom and I both knew, if the blue dress fit, I'd wear it. After all, there's no need to be practical when there'd probably be no next time.

In the dressing room, I put on the gown and thought, "I look beautiful ... but I look like Black-Tie Barbie." Grown-ups don't wear satiny baby blue, right? But this dress fit as though the designer woke up one morning and said, "I'm going to make a dress for Jen today." I had to have it.

The color made my blue eyes look even bluer. The length was just right with the perfect set of high heels to lift the dress off the ground. The fit accentuated the years I'd spent sweating off my baby fat in the gym. "That's the dress for you!" the saleswoman gushed as though she had discovered an unearthed source of gold. Mom smiled at me. This was, indeed, THE DRESS.

The night of the event, I appeared in our kitchen in my new blue gown. My babysitter gasped, "Oh, Mrs. Singer! That dress was made for you." Meanwhile, my six year old looked for the dress' train. Disappointed that Thomas The Tank Engine wasn't hanging from my, uh, caboose, he quickly lost interest.

But Pete had the same look that was on his face he had had when I walked down the aisle in my wedding gown. The next day, my Mickey Mouse shirt would go into the rag pile.

"Did the dress make you feel all princessey?" a friend later asked. Yes, it did. When we walked down Park Avenue toward the Waldorf, people in taxis stared. The taxi drivers even stared, and New York cabbies have seen it all.

In the hall outside the ballroom, a woman pulled me aside and said, "Way to go! Everyone's wearing black in there. You're really gonna stand out!" And I did. When I walked in, heads turned as though a celebrity had just entered the ballroom, and not "just" a stay-at-home mom.

Later, in the Ladies Room, two twenty-somethings in little black dresses gave me the once-over. I smirked at them and thought, "Someday girls, you, too, can be housewives in fabulous blue dresses You, too, can feel like Cinderella."

Later that night, I put my gown away in the back of my closet. But I haven't put away that feeling. I've been buying clothes that don't say, "I'm someone's mom": a pair of flared, tight fitting pants and cool black boots, a suede jacket with faux fur collar, a bikini with a matching sheer cover-up. And not one is a Large.

Mommy got her groove back, and it all started with a fabulous baby blue gown. If only I could wear it to pre-school pick-up.

Would You Apply for This Job?

Stay-at-Home Mother: Full-time position - must work upwards of fourteen hours a day or ninety-eight hours a week. Plus, on call all night, every night. No vacation days, no sick days, no coffee breaks, no lunch hour, unless you count holding baby with one arm while scarfing down your toddler's leftover grilled cheese crusts with the other.

No experience necessary, though it helps if you know that you need to add a degree if you take your child's temperature under his arm and that the cartoon characters on the diapers go in the front.

No chance for advancement, though you will eventually get to bring a magazine to the beach - and actually read it. Well, parts of it.

Math skills a plus, especially if you can quickly add in your head how many minutes until the baby will get REALLY hungry and, therefore, break into a piercing wail.

Must be able to handle extensive paperwork, including health-care forms, permission slips, bake sale flyers, and a dozen or so pieces of "I made it for you, Mommy" artwork that must be hung on the refrigerator door daily.

What little time you carve out without your charges will likely be spent bringing returns to Baby Gap and buying Scooby-Doo wrapping paper for your kid's pre-school classmate's birthday party.

Perks include: wearing sneakers or even slippers daily, watching *The Little Mermaid* on a rainy Tuesday afternoon and chewing bubble gum while on the job.

Starts after extensive nine-month training period during which you won't be able to pull yourself off the couch without assistance. Job continues until the last kid leaves for good - with your mini-van.

AFTERWORD

Since I started my web site for stay-at-home moms, www.MommaSaid.net, I've heard from thousands of mothers around the world who have said they thought they were the only ones who sometimes (or often times) felt exhausted, lonely, depressed and/or trapped as at-home moms. They said they'd been afraid to tell anyone, especially because staying home with your kids is seen as a privilege in today's economy. I told them they're not alone.

Taking care of small children fourteen-plus hours a day is often a tiring and thankless job. It's also a rewarding and important job, and therein lies the paradox. Before you become a mother, you think your days will be like a baby lotion commercial: lots of cooing and tender, loving moments and clean-smelling, happy babies. And sometimes it is.

But sometimes it's colic and blow-out diapers and exhaustion and despair and Play-Doh ground deep into your living room carpet. And on those days - and there will be many - it's perfectly okay not to enjoy being home with the kids. It's even okay to fantasize about going back to work or about going to Tahiti with Ashton Kutcher.

Stay-at-home parenting is a job, albeit an unpaid one. No one should be expected to work 24/7 with no vacation days, holidays or sick days - and yet we are. Everyone needs a break now and then, and

I don't mean a trip to the supermarket alone. I mean a real break: go to a movie with girlfriends, go on a date with your husband, take a morning to sleep in.

If you need an excuse to take time for yourself, take an actual holiday: MommaSaid's "Please Take My Children to Work Day," is held annually on the last Monday in June. I know I will. Maybe we can meet for coffee - without the kids.

Meanwhile, take care of yourself, because you can't tend to everyone else when you're absolutely spent. Nurture your passions and interests. Sleep whenever you can. Pat yourself on the back. And remember, you're a good mom. Really.

Momma Said there'd be days like this.
She just never said it'd be EVERY DAY.

Visit MommaSaid.net

We're the award-winning web site where full- and part-time at-home moms can drop by for some comic relief during their 14-hour days.

Stop by and see what everyone's talking about.

The Housewife Awards™ Bi-weekly awards for real-life desperate housewives. Isn't it time you got a pat on the back?

Momma-logues™ Video dispatches from the "hood" - stay-at-home motherhood. Rated G - no cursing, no violence and no "wardrobe malfunctions."

Discover lots of family funnies at MommaSaid.net.

- The Back Fence - Funny things that happen to Mom.

- Potties in Heaven - Kids say the darndest things.

- Just a Minute - Kids do the darndest things.

- While They're Little - Essays and funny bits on motherhood.

Stop by our Guest Room and share your stories.

- Momma Asked - Parenting questions from moms around the world.

- Momma Laughs - Funny parenting photos.

- Stupid Parenting Tricks - Silly things folks have done as parents.

- Seasoned Parents - Tips, thoughts and warnings from parents of older kids.

- Stump Mommy - Jen Singer's constant dilemma to answer her kids' unending questions,

Mom's on the Loose! A blog about *14 Hours 'Til Bedtime.*